A/E/C Marketing Fundamentals

Michael T. Kubal

J. A. Jones Construction Services
Charlotte, NC

Kevin T. Miller

Frost Miller Group Inc.
Bethesda, MD

Ronald D. Worth

Society for Marketing Professional Services
Washington, DC

The Society for Marketing Professional Services

Society for Marketing
Professional Services

99 Canal Center Plaza
Suite 330
Alexandria, VA 22314

BNi Building News

Editor-In-Chief
William D. Mahoney, P.E.

Technical Services
Ana Varela
Robert O. Wright

BNi PUBLICATIONS, INC.

LOS ANGELES
10801 National Blvd., Ste.100
Los Angeles, CA 90064

ANAHEIM
1612 S. Clementine St.
Anaheim, CA 92802

NEW ENGLAND
PO BOX 14527
East Providence, RI 02914

WASHINGTON, D.C.
502 Maple Ave. West
Vienna, VA 22180

1-888-BNi-BOOK
1-888-264-2665

ISBN 1-55701-483-3

A/E/C Marketing Fundamentals

This book was written by Michael T. Kubal, Kevin T. Miller, and Ronald D. Worth. Originally published by McGraw-Hill in 2000 as *Building Profits in the Construction Industry*. Revised, updated, and reprinted with permission from McGraw-Hill. Edited by S. Cutler and M. Doon.

Additional information can be obtained from BNi Publications, Inc.

Table of Contents

About the Authors

Michael T. Kubal is president of the Environmental Division, J. A. Jones Construction Co., in Washington, DC. He has extensive experience as a project manager of multimillion-dollar building projects, and as a supervisor of renovations and historic restorations. Kubal is the author of McGraw-Hill's *Waterproofing the Building Envelope* and *Engineering Quality in Construction*. He is also co-author of *Building Profits in the Construction Industry,* on which this book is based.

Kevin Miller is president and founder of the Frost Miller Group, a marketing communications firm based in Washington, DC, that represents a broad range of businesses nationwide. He was previously director of marketing communication for one of the nation's largest construction firms. Miller is co-author of *Building Profits in the Construction Industry*.

Ronald D. Worth is chief executive officer of the Society for Marketing Professional Services. Before this, he was executive vice president of the Washington Building Congress. He has, among other positions, worked coast to coast as director of marketing for a national construction services corporation. He is a lecturer and writer and serves on the boards of several national trade associations. Worth is co-author of *Building Profits in the Construction Industry*.

Introduction

Things change. This book meets the challenge of this change in marketing A/E/C services by providing marketers with the resources and ideas necessary to adapt to the numerous standards changing the A/E/C industry. But before we can do this, we must thoroughly understand how the A/E/C industry has changed in recent years, in order to meet the new marketing patterns of the 21st century. Equipped with basic knowledge of these electronic-age paradigms, an A/E/C marketer can tailor, develop, and formulate a structured marketing program that increases opportunities for success.

Organizations have become increasingly more marketing driven: everyone is now a salesperson. Aggressive contractors take the necessary steps to involve all their personnel in marketing, including superintendents who are trained to network with subcontractor representatives at the site for other sales opportunities. Project managers become experts in continuing relationships with existing clients. Even the accounting staff recognizes the importance of servicing customers to ensure a steady flow of repeat business. In fact, the more progressive marketing-driven companies in the A/E/C industry establish a marketing budget for every ongoing job site to facilitate marketing opportunities as they arise. Those companies that will continue to be successful in future decades will base the structure of their organizations on an environment of growth and constant renewal.

The idea of a market-driven culture for companies in the design and construction industries was almost unheard of just a few years ago. Today there exist national associations, such as the Associated General Contractors (AGC) and others, representing various facets of the A/E/C industry. A recent survey of AGC's membership highlighted the critical need to instill this "culture" within each member of the team, including those in the field, project managers, estimators, secretaries, and particularly any member who interfaces with the client on a regular basis. This is true in every facet of the A/E/C industry—engineering, architecture, construction, landscape design, interior design, or any professional services arena.

Progressive A/E/C firms of all types are effectively enhancing their culture to reflect the dynamics necessary to succeed in today's competitive environment. Today we are presented with a wealth of new opportunities in the preparation of a game plan that will minimize risks, provide solid direction, and lead companies to favorable results. The A/E/C industry must follow the trend of immediately gratified expectations and must compress the time to produce the finished product.

The new virtual-age principles have facilitated the growth in strategic alliances that enable contractors to target a wider variety of opportunities by increasing their capabilities without having to add to their existing resources. Alliances permit contractors to contract larger projects, using design-build contracts, in more expanded geographical areas than they would be able to without the alliance partnership.

Clearly, marketing is not what it used to be, and the intention of this book is to introduce marketers to the new realities of A/E/C marketing that enhance the successful marketing practices that have been standard for most of us for a very long time.

Chapter

1

21st Century Realities of A/E/C Services Marketing

Marketing, including marketing of A/E/C services, has changed substantially over the past few years. Marketing is now as likely to take place electronically as it is in person.

In earlier times, few marketers had access to e-mail, but today it is so vital to the communications element of business life that letters, contracts, brochures, and qualifications statements are sent electronically and can be received instantly by potential clients. With more and more companies now offering their employees access to e-mail, this has become a standard marketing resource. CDs and DVDs replace brochures, overhead presentations are now computer presentations, and oral presentations have morphed into video conferencing.

In fact, marketers can perform their services today without ever having to meet the customer face to face (hence the name: virtual marketing). For example, remote A/E/C marketers, regardless of their location, can interrelate with federal government representatives located in Washington, DC, electronically using the Internet. It is entirely possible that a sale can result without the customer ever having met personally with a contractor's representative.

Web pages and the Internet also have become standard marketing tools. Not only do customers have their own web sites from which marketers can gain new insight into their companies, but also every major contractor now has a web site to transmit marketing information to anyone in the world.

Basic new concepts

Several new paradigms have changed the way A/E/C services are marketed. These paradigms, for the most part, were driven by the customer's perspective and requirements. These new concepts must be adapted into any strategic marketing strategy for an A/E/C marketing program to be successful:

- the global village
- electronic capabilities
- commodity services
- bonding rather than selling
- risk transference
- time compression
- partnering

The global village

The ability to communicate directly to any destination from any source electronically has created a global village, and for many domestic general contractors, it has created an opportunity for entry into foreign markets. Today, millions of dollars of domestic design billings are derived from foreign projects. At the same time, foreign firms have captured millions of dollars worth of domestic billings in the United States, and this business will continue to grow, especially in the technology design fields.

This two-way paradigm means opportunity as well as a threat to a company's existing business. Domestic firms not already owned by foreign corporations are eagerly teaming, partnering, and forming strategic alliances with them to compete more effectively. This global village paradigm is prompting the industry to hire more foreign-speaking and foreign-educated professionals to increase their domestic in-house capabilities and facilitate competition abroad. Competition is no longer just local; it is now global as well.

The global village, in combination with electronic connectivity, enables individuals to work in real time with anyone around the world. This capability permits engineering firms to bring the best available talent to a project regardless of a person's location. It permits organizations to staff *virtually*—bringing talent to a project only as necessary without having to maintain a completely diverse full-time staff capable of completing all disciplines of engineering and architecture.

Furthermore, clients no longer must settle for the best available "local" talent; they can now have their designs completed by architectural or engineering companies around the world as if the firm was "just around the block." Today, when you pick up your telephone, you don't know if the call is coming from Cincinnati or Singapore. Goods and services come from everywhere—Malibu, Timbuktu, or Hong Kong. The world has truly become a global village, and the implications of this trend have penetrated well into the A/E/C industries, changing forever how work is marketed, sold, and completed.

Electronic capabilities

Computer hardware and software have revolutionized the way business is conducted in the A/E/C profession as well as in the companies of the industry's clients. Most work processes have been computerized as stand-alone improvements. In the construction and design industry, the most effective improvements cannot be implemented until all team members are capable of connecting electronically to share all project-related files.

Connectivity between team members is necessary to make full and effective use of computer hardware processing capability and instant communications through networks. Advancements in computer connectivity have facilitated vast improvements in managing the entire construction process.

Commodity services

Today's design and construction profession is frequently treated as a commodity service, despite the fact that professionals have ultimate control over the client's total direct costs of building. Architects and engineers often exert the greatest influence on costs expended during the construction phase. The design team is often followed by the contractor or construction manager in descending order of influence on overall cost control.

Unfortunately, clients often place too much emphasis on the fees charged by these professionals when actually their costs in comparison to the project's overall costs are minuscule. Averages of a wide range of projects reveal that designing and construction management fees generally represent less than ten percent of total building costs. The remaining 90 percent is directly attributable to hard, or direct cost of construction. During the early stages of a project, including the selection of team professionals, clients must be cautioned to place an emphasis on value and not merely on price.

However, given the current trend toward commodity pricing, that is exactly what frequently happens. Spurred on by fierce competition and the need to reduce operating costs and increase profits, commodity pricing has spread from department stores such as Wal-Mart to medicine (HMOs), law, and construction. Commodity pricing is fine for assembly-line products but not for services *that require human beings to exercise critical thinking.* You may not care if your hamburger comes from McDonald's or Burger King, for instance, but you surely care whether your family physician has a medical degree.

Architecture, engineering, and construction management are not off-the-shelf products that can be packaged and sold like widgets. They are highly specialized, thought-intensive services that must be specially tailored to each construction project. Unfortunately, the pressure to compete at the lowest common denominator has led many owners to regard these services as mere commodities and to base their selections on low prices from a short list of firms that meet minimum qualifications. Rarely do these owners realize the ramifications of forcing inadequate fees on design and construction professionals, who must limit their services and investment in a particular project to remain profitable and competitive.

If your intrinsic thinking on cost versus quality is still in that *traditional mode,* ask yourself a question. On your next airline flight to anywhere, sit down in your seat and say to yourself, "John (or whatever your name is), have you realized that this plane was designed and built by the lowest bidder?"

DNA

That is why it is so often incumbent upon A/E/C marketers to "sell" the owner of a project on the virtues of a firm's ability to control overall project costs in addition to providing quality work, which is, of course, paramount. The following are some points about which a marketer should make potential clients aware:

1. Successful cost control on an A/E/C project is the result of teamwork by all involved parties. To increase value for the owner, you must ensure that all team members are working toward the same goals. They must not be preoccupied with maintaining their profitability due to pricing *services* as a *commodity*.

2. If fees are higher, but they include services to better manage overall costs and quality, the owner may benefit by spending more in the initial stages of a project in order to reduce costs in the field construction stage.

3. *Employees* make a firm, not vice versa. In A/E/C services, the issue of costs generally comes down to paying greater fees for greater talent and additional services. The people selected for a project will ultimately make the project a success or failure, not the *companies* themselves. Selecting a firm that offers lower costs often means the client might be served by less capable professionals or by entry-level employees. This ultimately will result in *increased* overall project costs and *lower* quality. Again, rather than focusing on price, the owner should be looking for value. Ask yourself: What type of experience does the firm have, and what are the credentials of the people who have been assigned to this project?

4. The firm or companies selected should guarantee that no "bait and switch" of employees will occur after the contract award. All too often, to meet commodity pricing of services, organizations will submit qualified candidate resumes, and then switch to lower-level and less-skilled employees to maintain or increase their minimal commodity-priced profit margins. This can have a serious impact on the result.

5. Most importantly, professional services should not be sold as a commodity. Marketers are responsible for convincing potential clients that experienced professionals deserve serious value considerations. Clients will defer pricing issues only if they perceive in your proposal getting better value than they would from competitors. After all, one seldom gets the best for less.

Bonding rather than selling

An era of business relationships that transcends supplier and customer negotiations simply for the best price or service has become increasingly common. The age of the global village concept requires that everyone actively seeking a business relationship surpass all previously established standard practices, even beyond partnering, to earn a potential client's business. The new global economy is changing forever the way business is initially attracted and retained, with an emphasis on bonding with clients and customers.

Private owners and major corporations have now begun to align their facility objectives with their business objectives. Today, acquired real estate holdings either become profit centers in themselves or the holdings are managed at the lowest possible costs to prevent deterioration of corporate profitability. The A/E/C industry must respond to these new realities and implement the programs necessary to facilitate the aligning of facility needs with the client's business objectives.

Design teams spend the time necessary to help a client review multiple sites for adaptability to their physical plant requirements before any conceptual designs are begun. Contractors supply pre-construction services well in advance of these conceptual designs, providing estimates of construction costs based on "statement of need" parameters.

Additionally, all team members may be asked to participate financially in the future success of their client, deferring some of their initial fees and compensation for possible profit sharing after the client becomes established. As more and more communities offer financing to lure business to their areas, the contractor is likely to be required to participate in the assurances to facilitate the sale of industrial revenue bonds.

This process takes time and financial commitments from the contractor to ensure completion of the project at the start of bond interest earning. The architectural team must design within the bond sale revenue, and all team members must contain the final product costs within these parameters. Such public-private partnerships are becoming increasingly common.

Commitments for assistance not only start earlier but end later as well. Post-construction services are now common, particularly among manufacturing clients who demand that the entire building team participate in the turnover and start-up stage of their operations to ensure a smooth transition to the profit-making stage of all projects. Clearly, the trends indicate a leaning toward performance contracts in construction rather than only completion of a building to plans and specifications.

In the next decade, real estate, design, and construction professionals will become more actively involved in the ongoing success of their clients' operations to ensure the success of their own organizations. Relationships that lead to future business opportunities begin earlier than ever before, when the client begins strategic planning for a construction requirement that is years away. Successful marketers become partners, not just vendors.

Risk transference

During the past decade, construction industry customers increased their use of risk transference to other parties, typically through legal advisement. Transferring risk was presumed to be an effective contractual means to reduce exposure to risk during a project's construction by assuring that an owner would not have to pay for this risk allocation.

In reality, though, the opposite effect occurs. Architects and contractors attempt to transfer their assumption of risk to their subcontractors and consultants. Moreover, parties attempt to apply increased compensation costs to assume risk, thereby increasing overall project costs.

Appropriately, risks associated with professional services should be retained by the organization being paid to complete these services. This is particularly true for all risks associated with construction designs. In the typical design-bid-build contracting method, the owner is required to assume all risks associated with the preparation of the drawings and specifications, guaranteeing to the contractor that the design is free of errors and omissions. Recently, clients have realized they should not have to retain or attempt to transfer design risks, but rather design risk should be retained by the architectural and engineering firms that are paid a fee for these professional services.

This situation has led to the substantial increase in design-build projects in the past decade. Design-build contracting assures clients that all professional risks associated with the design are retained by the construction professional. Using the design-build contract format, the owner is relieved of having to guarantee the design documents to the contractor, who is now directly responsible for these documents.

Marketers should be aware of how and when risk should be transferred and should be sufficiently experienced in these issues to know when a potential client is requiring the contractor to assume too much risk to ensure a profitable project. Risk, in fact, should be allocated to the party who is in the best position to account for and manage the risk. For example, general contractors are best able to deal with labor issues, architects with building codes, and owners with existing and unforeseen site conditions.

Many common contract clauses attempt to transfer risk to other team members. Those more frequently used include the following:

1. *No damages for delay.* An owner or architectural firm that causes a delay is not responsible for any costs or damages related to the delay, including those due to time delays and related extended general conditions costs.

2. *Indemnification.* Recent transference attempts include the complete indemnity of clients and architects for any actions they might cause. The contractor is expected to assume the risk by contract obligations regardless of whether an accident is caused in whole or in part by something with which the contractor had absolutely no involvement.

3. *Environmental impacts.* Often, existing and unforeseen site conditions arising from environmental conditions are transferred to the general contractor, such as soil contamination from underground petroleum storage tanks.

4. *Pay if paid.* A contractor might include contract language that attempts to avoid having to pay a subcontractor or supplier if the contractor does not first receive payment from the client.

5. *Actual damages.* Owners require that contractors and designers assume all possible costs associated with delays in project completion without regard to the amount of fee and profit opportunity involved.

6. *Design responsibility.* Design team members attempt to pass design responsibility on to contractors and subcontractors through specification clauses. An example is the mechanical and electrical design coordination with architectural and structural plans that may be in conflict with each other through the design team's fault.

7. *Existing site conditions.* These include subsurface and unforeseen site conditions, the most frequent being rock and underground water, for which the client attempts to have the general contractor assume responsibility.

Marketers should have a clear understanding of the types of risks involved in construction and their organizations' regulations pertaining to the assumption of this risk. In addition, marketers should be able to detail to potential clients the professional team members best capable of dealing with the various types of risks involved in construction.

All members of the project team benefit by establishing a win-win contractual relationship. Clients receive a fair price for work contracted, all parties are able to complete the project without unnecessary conflicts, and overall quality and time standards are increased in the process.

Time compression

Consumers today demand instant gratification. Products and services are now customized and delivered immediately, if not sooner. Because manufacturers and service providers have to contend with this instant paradigm in their own industries, they in turn expect the construction industry to respond in a like manner.

Although no building or facility can be completed instantly, clients are now demanding that contractors and designers greatly compress overall design and construction schedules so that they, in turn, can compete effectively in their own industries. A/E/C marketers must be aware of these time expectations and be able to confidently present their company's qualifications and capabilities to meet the particular requirements.

We will review this time paradigm in detail, including how the industry's leading companies approach advancing their project scheduling compression utilizing techniques such as virtual scheduling.

Partnering

Although not unique to the construction or design profession, partnering has become an industry standard for improving a project's overall quality and reducing the number of disputes and litigation that occur over the course of constructing a project. Partnering usually describes the formation of a project team that has a set of common goals in addition to each individual company's goals.

Partnering is not a legal or contractual obligation. In a way, it is a return to the "old fashioned" way of doing business and to the basics in business relationships. It restores trust in business agreements and opens once-closed avenues of communication. It creates a team environment in which to accomplish a set of goals in much the same way a sports team works together to achieve its goals. Using the partnering concept, individuals learn to respect other team members' roles in the project and recognize the inherent risks associated with their professional responsibilities.

Partnering ultimately results in more successful business relationships and less dependency upon legal assistance. It allows project team members to once again accept their individual responsibilities, with all other team members supporting those responsibilities.

Partnering has been a success and has become a standard in the A/E/C industry because the ultimate success of any project or company is due to its employees. Partnering builds the teamwork necessary to permit each person to obtain the assistance needed to be successful—individually and collectively as a team. Partnering promotes the following improvement goals:

- ◆ open communication
- ◆ profitability of all team members
- ◆ improved (compressed) schedules
- ◆ enhanced safety program
- ◆ better business relationships
- ◆ innovations
- ◆ reductions in or elimination of dependence upon outside legal assistance
- ◆ increased levels of trust among both individuals and companies

Marketers should be fully informed of the partnering process and be able to explain and promote the process to all prospective customers. Companies that promote the involvement of their marketing team with clients before, during, and after a project's completion should involve the marketer in the actual partnering process itself. Marketers can monitor the process to ensure that clients' goals are highlighted in the partnering sessions and that an open line of communication with customers is maintained.

Although this section does not provide a complete review of the partnering process, it gives a general description of it for those unfamiliar with the process. A/E/C partnering most often begins with a partnering session after all the major team members involved in a project are selected. The earlier in the overall design and construction process that partnering begins, the more likely it is to be successful. For example, clients who begin partnering in the design phase with contractor involvement can expect greater benefits from the process than from partnering that begins after the design is completed.

There are several steps necessary to start the process leading to a partnering agreement for a particular project. The first step is the completion of a partnering session that includes numerous components:

1. The individual team members make each other aware of their individual goals.
2. The team defines the common objective(s).
3. They develop a structured program to determine how to cooperate to reach individual and common goals.
4. The team establishes a method of accountability, measurement, and evaluation of these goals.
5. They establish open communications (including complete electronic connectivity) to resolve problems before they become disputes.

Partnering does not end with this initial session; it must be renewed constantly to maintain interest in the program so that it will eventually lead to a successful project for all team members. Team members should establish a schedule of partnering sessions throughout the project's duration to ensure that the effort is renewed and continually updated so as to monitor the progress and the objective of reaching the goals established in the initial session.

Communication is the single most important principle of partnering agreements. Today, partnering is based on the ability to link together all team members electronically to facilitate instant communication, vastly improving the ability to meet and exceed partnering goals more than ever before. For example, project time schedules, which clients now rank as one of their hottest issues, can be greatly improved by team members monitoring them and providing input about them on a continuing basis instead of the past methods of monthly or weekly meetings to review schedules.

Summarizing the goals of both the individuals and the team as a whole is the outcome of the initial partnering session. These goals are then set forth in a partnering document much like an agreement of work ethics formerly sealed by a handshake. A sample partnering agreement is shown in **Figure 1.1**. Copies of the document are distributed to all team members.

All marketers should be fully aware of partnering and their management's attitude toward and support of the process. This partnering paradigm will take on even more significance when the industry fully implements electronic connectivity of all team members to improve the quality of the finished product that will be produced rapidly to meet the customer's requirements.

Marketing Principles That Will Never Change

Although marketing has changed and will continue to change in the age of electronic communication, some standard principles will never change, especially those relating to customer relationships. How we contact and communicate with a customer may have changed dramatically, but the manner in which customers should be treated will never change. Before moving on to the current world of marketing, we will review several enduring marketing techniques: (1) marketing versus sales; (2) perception is everything; (3) some customers are best ignored; (4) treat clients as friends; and (5) know your customer

We, the team members for the _____ (project name) are dedicated to achieving the quality standards defined by the contract documents, including plans and specifications). The quality standards and goals of this project will be achieved through our commitment to providing a safe and clean environment with zero lost-time accidents, open communication, and specific problem resolution guidelines to eliminate all potential disputes. It is our intention to succeed in each of the following segments of working conditions.

Open Communication
- Ensure that each team member maintains honest and open communication
- Maintain an open-door office policy
- Attend project meetings regularly
- Instill this philosophy in all other project participants
- Attend all additional partnering sessions

Conflict Resolution
- Resolve issues at the lowest level or the level at which the problem arises
- Problems not resolvable at this level shall be reported to the next level of project management
- Problems not resolved at the project management level will be grouped and concisely reported to upper management
- Contract documents shall govern the resolution of all problems not resolved by the partnering agreement
- Litigation and other legal assistance shall be avoided at all costs

Safety
- Complete the project with zero lost-time accidents
- Insist on a clean work site every day
- All team members shall participate in the safety program and attend appropriate safety meetings
- Involve safety inspectors, including OSHA, on a proactive basis rather than a penalty basis

Performance Measurement
- Zero lost-time accidents
- Complete project with no outstanding disputes
- Finish on or before scheduled completion date
- No punch list at substantial completion
- All warranties, as-built drawings, and maintenance booklets delivered to owner by final completion
- Maintain weekly updates of project schedule
- No warranty returns to project
- Change requests, RFIs, and other information requests to be resolved within one week of initial submittal
- All shop drawings approved per limits set by contract
- Change requests limited to 3 percent of contract amount
- Follow-up Workshops

It is further intended that additional partnering workshops be held to introduce new members of the project team to the commitments above. At minimum, these follow-up workshops will be held:
- At completion of project documents
- After selection of trade contractors
- At 33 percent completion
- At 67 percent completion

Figure 1.1. Sample partnering agreement.

It is further agreed that after the successful completion of this project, we will all meet to celebrate its conclusion.

We, the undersigned, are committed to put forth our best efforts to implement this program, with each member acting individually in the best interests of the entire team.

OWNER _____

CONTRACTOR _____

MAJOR SUBCONTRACTORS _____

_____

CONSULTANTS/INSPECTORS _____

_____

_____

Figure 1.1. Continued.

Marketing versus sales

There is a difference between marketing and sales even though many A/E/C companies manage them as one operation, usually within the business development department. Although the same employee can be responsible for both marketing and sales, management and the business development staff should recognize the differences between the two functions.

The new realities of A/E/C construction services demand that a contractor maintain not only the standard estimating department but, at minimum, a sales or business development staff that has the ability to perform marketing functions to increase the number of opportunities identified for sale closure.

Although most dictionaries define marketing as the act or process of sales, in a technical sense, there is a difference between marketing and sales. The best way to describe this intended difference is to use an analogy: If marketing is a war, sales are individual battles during an ongoing war.

Marketing is the plan of attack or road map that succinctly develops the program a contractor intends to follow during a certain period of time. Marketing becomes the process that develops the sales contacts that turn into contracts. Marketing is general; sales are specific. A marketing program includes planning to attract business opportunities in a new geographical area or specific type of work and is structured to result ultimately in specific sales opportunities.

Marketing is the process that attracts customers to inquire into a practitioner's capabilities, with the sales effort being the contact with the specific potential customers identified by the marketing process. Marketing programs include planning processes that position a company to be recognized as a solution for its targeted client's needs. Once identified as a possible solution, the company's sales process begins selling the company's services to this identified client.

Specifically in design professional services, marketing would begin with a strategic plan and mission statement that structures a program to communicate to prospective clients. The process then reverts to a specific sales opportunity when a contractor receives an inquiry from a potential client. For an engineer, architect, contractor, or any other person involved in providing professional services, establishing a direct-marketing mailing program to satisfy a requirement of a strategic plan is a marketing process. Preparing a proposal for a client responding to this mailing is the sales process. The contact with this client between the initial response and the request for proposal is likely to be a combination of marketing processes: providing a general qualifications package to supply further information, and probably a personal sales call regarding the client's planned building project. As there are many aspects of marketing, one can take this many steps further. Any contact with a client or potential client is a marketing task, even if it is the receptionist's handling of a telephone call, or the accounting department's sending an invoice.

The line between marketing and sales often becomes blurred. Essentially there is nothing wrong when this occurs because effective marketing programs should evolve into sales calls. Everyone in business development should recognize that ultimately marketing and sales are both used to increase sales opportunities for the company. Many A/E/C firms have no marketing programs, relying instead on a sales effort that unfortunately too often exists only as an estimating department.

Although it is not mandatory for a small general contractor, for instance, to create a separate marketing and sales department, it should be understood that effective sales calls begin with a clearly defined marketing program that identifies a customer as appropriate for the company's long-term success goals. It must also be understood by the employees of an A/E/C firm, or any firm offering professional services, that every person working for that firm should be considered a marketer.

Perception is everything

The way a person or company is perceived has always been a critical factor for successful marketing programs. In today's virtual society, perception is even more important. In fact, it means everything.

The Internet has created an environment where a person can be anyone he or she wants to be by communicating electronically the information that will form the desired perceptions. The Internet allows children to be perceived as adults, adults as children, and nonexistent companies as companies.

The age of electronic communication has created what is referred to as the virtual organization, a company that exists only to complete a certain task; it then dissolves and is re-created when another need arises. In effect, by establishing a web site, a person can create a company through posted documentation but have no employees or experience. This kind of company will hire temporary workers only when an order is received from a client. Otherwise, the company does not physically exist, even though potential clients of this *virtual* company perceive it as an actual operating entity.

Marketing is constantly used to create favorable perceptions. Today "spin doctors" have become common in politics. These people are actually marketers communicating their side of the story, slanting it in the most positive light possible to create a favorable perception by the public. Spin doctors use faxes, e-mail, and other forms of communication to spread their side of the story as quickly as possible, because often the first information received by people forms the basis of their perception of the facts.

Perceptions can be based on fact or fiction, and individuals can perceive another person or company any way they please. The perception, once formed, is very difficult to change, regardless of whether it is right or wrong. For example, a person might make a first visit to a department store, be treated unkindly, and conclude that this entire department store chain is poorly managed based upon this one encounter. It is very unlikely that this perception will ever be changed.

The same person might express this view to others who have not visited the store, and influence their attitude toward the store before they have even had an opportunity to form their individual opinions. This emphasizes the recognized fact that although a satisfied customer might not generate more business, a dissatisfied customer can cause a serious loss in revenue simply because people are more likely to communicate their disappointment than their approval. You've heard the statement that a dissatisfied customer will tell ten people who will tell ten people who will tell ten people... Take the risk of poor service, and before you know it, your reputation as a company to be avoided will have traveled far and wide.

As with all other industries, perceptions about A/E/C contractors are common. Unfortunately for the industry, too many clients think A/E/C contractors are change-order driven. In fact, most contractors believe that change orders are not sufficiently profitable to emphasize them, and most would prefer projects be completed without any change requests.

A marketer establishes the proper perception about a company by communicating, using the numerous means of communications available today, and should be able to effectively communicate a positive perception to everyone. Consider the following example.

There are two contractors named *Good* and *Bad*. Both have sold similar projects to similar customers. Almost immediately, after start of field construction, both *Bad* and *Good* experience problems on their projects. *Bad,* on his own initiative, takes immediate steps to correct each problem as it occurs. *Good* also takes immediate corrective measures. However, *Bad* fails to maintain effective communication with the owner through the company's marketer or project manager.

Although *Bad* is trying to correct the problem, the client recognizes only that problems continue to arise on the project. *Good*, however, has established an effective marketing program that includes defined steps to maintain continuous communication with the client. *Good's* marketer continues to relay to the client that although problems may occur, *Good* rises to the occasion by taking immediate steps to correct the difficult situation despite "the problems caused by subcontractors." *Good's* client feels satisfied that he selected the right contractor, because *Good* is obviously taking care of his needs.

Bad has also taken the same steps. However, *Bad's* client runs into *Good's* client, and complains to him about how stressful it is working with *Bad* and dealing with continual problems on the project. *Good's* client recommends that his friend should try using *Good's* company for his next project because that company knows how to take care of problems.

importance of customer "Experience"

Presented with the same situation, both contractors are doing what is right, but one ends up with a negative review, whereas the other gets a positive review and a referral to a new client. The difference is perception. Both companies should have been perceived equally, but *Bad* was not regarded in a favorable light simply because it failed to communicate with the client and put the proper "spin" on the situation.

This example emphasizes the mandatory requirement of maintaining continued communication with clients to ensure that they receive constant and consistent information and ultimately the right impression. Too few contractors recognize that marketing is a continuous effort, not only to attract new clients, but to maintain existing clients. Aggressive and effective marketing programs include marketing training for project managers and superintendents so that they learn to communicate effectively with their clients. Most managers and superintendents can manage and communicate with subcontractors and suppliers, but few are trained to communicate with clients.

For perceptions to be positive and projects to be considered successful on completion, the contractor must recognize that marketing is a continuing process that cannot be ignored. Communication with clients through established contact with the marketer, and additional visits when deemed necessary, are critical in creating a positive perception in the marketplace, a perception that will lead to the future success of the company.

Some customers are best ignored

In every business, there are customers whose patronage a company is better off doing without. Every marketer should be able to recognize when it is appropriate to discontinue marketing to a specific client and abandon attempts to finalize a sale.

Too often, a sale is completed even though the marketing or sales representative recognizes that this client will probably not benefit the company and should not be solicited for contracting opportunities. Be wary of clients who (1) emphasize price only; (2) fail to recognize the value of services provided; (3) have a history of litigation; create a hostile work environment; (4) have insufficient financial resources; (5) have insufficient work experience; or (6) try to transfer too much risk from the owner to the contractor.

Clients who *emphasize price only* will never become repeat clients because every project they contract for is selected on the basis of low bid and low price. Although many contractors depend on low-bid work, a marketer should not waste company resources and funds to market to a client who is interested only in price and not quality.

The federal government is a perfect example of such a client. Many companies have made it a point not to waste marketing budgets on this potential client because of its dependence on a low-bid selection process, while ignoring a contractor's qualifications. Even though the federal government no longer depends on this selection method, many commercial customers still think they can take advantage of an industry in which it is easy to believe one can estimate the cost of a project that may be entirely new and for which there is no precedent.

Clients can certainly use low-bid contracting effectively to pre-qualify A/E/C companies, but those industry clients who are interested only in "getting something for nothing" are best left to competitors. Marketers should recognize that potential clients preoccupied with price issues never produce profitable long-term business relationships for a contractor. These clients *fail to recognize the value of services provided* and treat professional services as a commodity. Be wary of the client who is unaware of the value of professional services.

The clients we speak of also are likely to *create a hostile work environment.* They not only minimize the importance of the project and the skill it takes to create it, but also take for granted the value of the human beings who are responsible for designing, building, administering, and completing the project. So poor is their regard for the people involved, they think nothing of changing the scope of the project at various stages of completion. Thus, change requests instituted by the client become extensive and unprofitable bargaining sessions that ultimately prevent the contractor from making a reasonable profit.

It should be mandatory for every marketer to investigate and confirm the ability of a client to supply the *necessary financial resources* to complete the project successfully. Spending company time and resources to market to a client who has limited financial resources and is incapable of bringing a planned project to completion results in wasted time and effort for the marketer.

As early as possible, the marketer should determine the client's financial commitments to the project. It is not unreasonable to inquire into the financial support for the planned project before investing estimating time, pre-construction services, and other support requested by the client.

Marketers should be prepared to decide if the company they represent has the capacity and experience to satisfactorily complete work for the client and finance it during an extended process. Large corporate clients and others often do not recognize the need to pay promptly at stated intervals throughout the progress of the project. This, of course, must be spelled out when the initial contract is written: Payment is to be made at regular intervals as specific parts of the project reach completion. What the client must realize is that the contractor has invested money in materials and salaries for labor. If the project takes several years to complete, and the contractor isn't paid until after the project is complete, the contractor is in effect financing the project to the tune of millions of dollars. The contractor may not have the financial capacity to support or fund a large project indefinitely. Although a large corporate client might appear to be a good financial risk, poor payment policies or bureaucratic structures that impede payment are situations the marketer should bring to management's attention. Unless the customer can provide adequate guarantees of prompt payment and support during the construction, the business opportunity should be declined. (Any newspaper you pick up will give you examples of companies that folded in the middle of a project, leaving contractors in serious difficulties, even facing bankruptcy. Keep your eyes open. Don't put yourself in that position!)

Many clients, including the federal government, have begun to *attempt to transfer as much risk to the contractor as possible.* Projects are being advertised as design-build that in reality are already completely designed, with the client interested only in having the design risk transferred to the contractor. These so-called design-build projects require only the completion of some minor detailing or minimal design input such as landscaping design. This facade is then used to structure a design-build contract with the actual intention of transferring all document guarantee risk completely to the contractor, while maintaining control of the project's design.

Clients may also use extensive legal support to transfer all risks to the contractor through the contract and specifications. Marketers must use all resources available to them, including legal reviews, to ensure that the project can be completed without being overly burdened with the risk factor, and ultimately professional liability costs.

All too often, marketers do not think of qualifying the potential customer, which is an important requirement. Any marketer or salesperson is, of course, intensely focused on "making the sale." Who wouldn't be? However, it is dangerous to be so "hungry" for the sale that one overlooks the possibility of one "going sour." It is important to the success of any company for its representatives to recognize a good opportunity as well as the possibility of negative situations. The negative impact from just one financially bad project can negate the success of several good projects. The margins in A/E/C projects are too small to take unnecessary risks, and expert marketers are just as capable of rejecting risky opportunities as they are of closing good sales. One huge loss can put a company out of business!

Here's where networking comes in. Talk to friends. Without revealing your personal interest in this company as a client for your employer, see what you can find out about this potential client. Does he interfere with the crew? Does he complain too often? Does he pay his bills? Is he fair?

Treat clients as friends

Remember always that people buy from friends or people they know and trust. Competition doesn't take place only on technical skills, price, and experience levels. Very often, a sale is made because of past friendship. Friendship counts. In fact, it wires the job!

Marketers should recognize that marketing begins well before a project is planned or announced to the public. Clients are more apt to deal with contractors with whom they have forged a relationship based on previous knowledge of their needs, and with whom they have previously worked. Marketers who can create a good working relationship with the client will certainly be awarded the majority of that client's work, even in situations in which multiple proposals must be solicited in order to satisfy corporate regulations.

Successful marketing is not just submitting the best proposal; the best marketers recognize that many projects are sold long before the proposals are submitted. Use strategic planning to identify potential clients; then build a friendly relationship with them to earn their trust. Do this *before* you submit proposals. That is the key to successful marketing relationships.

If you want to establish a relationship based on trust and friendship, you should abide by five very specific rules of successful marketing:

1. *Never forget a customer or let a customer forget you.* Marketing is based on consistent renewal of existing relationships and on forging new ones. Through the process of personal contact, mailings, calls, and electronic marketing, marketers must remind customers about the A/E/C contractor's ability to help them achieve their goals. Marketers should never give the impression that they have abandoned the client once the bid has been accepted. A marketer should keep in constant contact with every existing client throughout the entire project process. A marketer should expect customer relationships to be maintained by the project manager as well. The marketer should be the resource to the client in the event of a problem. The client must also be given alternative contacts within the practitioner's organization to ensure that communications are always open. *(Here's my cell phone number if you need me. If, by chance, I am not available, call Marjorie at the main office.)* This creates the impression that the marketer is always available to support the client, establishing confidence, and ensuring that this solid relationship might lead to another project later. Abandon or ignore the client as soon as you've made the sale, and you risk your and the company's future!

2. *Take care of your clients and they will take care of you.* When clients believe they are being treated fairly and professionally, they are likely to return that treatment to the practitioner. Remember these adages: What goes around comes around. Don't burn your bridges.

A bad relationship can hurt you forever. Suddenly, in a new project, you came face to face with an old client with whom you have parted on a sour note. Be absolutely certain that client will make a remark to someone standing nearby. And the old disappointment will rankle for a very long time. Most clients belong to industry associations where they exchange information with others. No marketer wants a past client to repeatedly spread negative valuations to potential future clients, either when they are networking with their peers or when they have been contacted as a reference in qualification and technical submittals to a prospective client. That unhappy relationship will have its repercussions forever and a day. You may never hear the end of it. Placate that client no matter what you have to do. Set up a meeting. If you don't know, ask the past client what he is feeling and why. Do what you have to do to make him/her feel better. If an apology is required, make it. If some recompense is required, do what you can to make it.

The client is generally the CEO, or owner of the company; but the rancor may linger within his organization, among the rank and file. Courtesy by you is required from the top down.

This same treatment is expected for each specific contact within a client's organization. Should you have a clash with an employee in the client's firm, you may never be able to close a sale in that organization. Receptionists, secretaries, administrative assistants, accounting personnel, and others may have remarkable influence on their bosses. Marketers must commit to taking whatever steps are necessary to maintain a friendly relationship with the client and all the client's representatives. If the marketer gets the impression that a particular contact relationship within the client's organization is not working out, he or she should immediately find someone else in the organization to become the point of contact. Bad relationships do not result in sales.

3. *Existing clients are the best source of new business.* A satisfied client should be used as a reliable source of new business leads. Often a present client will give you potential sales leads just for the asking. Clients are certainly aware of their competitors and what is happening in the industry, and this information can help you learn which companies might be planning new projects, expansions, or renovations, sometimes long before they are publicly announced.

In addition, clients can also provide information on contacts within another organization through friendships and business associations. A referral or personal introduction can immediately open doors and form stronger relationships that might not otherwise occur.

At the very least, a satisfied existing client can be used as a reference to gain entry and business from other potential clients. Never forget the opportunities that a present customer can provide beyond work with his/her own organization. To be effective, you should use these relationships strategically to create other relationships and generate more business.

That's called *networking*, and it has been the lifeblood of business and all relationships from the beginning of time. Mankind could never have developed and created civilization without working together, using each other's capabilities, knowledge, and network of friends. You should use them, too.

4. *Never forget the word "thanks."* Too often marketers in their zealousness to close a sale and move on to the next potential lead forget to thank a client for awarding the project to his/her firm. Never forget to express the company's appreciation for the contract. Make sure the client recognizes that you will be available throughout the project's progress and you should continue to follow through with the client to ensure that the he or she is satisfied with the services provided. *("Thank you for the opportunity to serve your company. Speaking for my company and myself, I'd like to assure you that it is important to us in many ways to be part of a project that will make a difference to you, to us, and to the community. Count on us to follow through from beginning to end.")*

Everyone respects and appreciates working with people who are sincere about expressing gratitude for the opportunity provided. Even if a practitioner should not be successful in obtaining a particular contract, sending a letter of thanks is greatly appreciated by the client, who will certainly remember this when it's time for the next project. Never leave the client with the impression that the contractor did not appreciate the invitation to compete for the business. Note that in today's world this courteous gesture is seldom practiced by most professionals, in fact, by most people, and if you do so, it will ensure that you will stand out from the crowd.

A simple handwritten note of thanks is still preferred over an e-mail message. A marketer should frequently send thank you notes to those who provide leads, information, or direct business opportunities. Sincere appreciation is most likely to result in future opportunities. This is one point that will go a long way to establish you in the mind of a prospective client as a friend or partner. Take this one step further, if you want to boost your career to the very highest level as a professional and as a marketer: When you see an article or notice in a newspaper or other periodical that will affect this client (or any other with whom you do business), clip it, put it into an envelope, and send it to him/her with a handwritten note. "I thought this might be of interest to you." Watch your reputation as a professional and valued friend zoom!

5. *Reciprocate whenever possible.* Everyone is in business to make a profit. Marketers must recognize that their clients are also required to sell work to stay in business. Marketers, whenever possible, should pass on appropriate leads or business opportunities to their clients. Nothing can cement a relationship better than providing a business opportunity for a client, or

anyone you know in business. Sharing information makes you important to the other person as much as he/she is important to you.

Likewise, marketers should keep this in mind for those they use as network sources for sharing leads. No one will continue to share leads and information with people who do not reciprocate. Passing on information when appropriate is an important part of marketing or any business relationship. It permits the establishment of a network group that is crucial to the success of any marketing program.

These simple marketing practices can create a solid foundation of success for any marketer. The philosophy behind these principles is that to succeed, you must remember those who are responsible for your success. While you are the driving force in your own life, without the acceptance of your clients with respect to your efforts, you go nowhere in this market (or for that matter, in any work environment).

Know your customer

Just as important as establishing effective relationships with customers by getting to know them on an individual basis is gaining knowledge of their business and future goals. Helping a client become successful is the ultimate goal of any marketing program and in turn helps the marketers achieve their companies' own goals.

Only by spending the time and effort necessary to learn a client's goals and requirements can you provide the assistance that results in long-term relationships. Meeting with a prospect only to boast of your firm's capabilities is useless. He/she can easily learn what your capabilities are. The question in his mind is can you solve his problems? Can you find solutions to a dilemma? Can you achieve what she has in mind? Can you envision the goal he sees? You must emphasize the value of services your company can provide rather than emphasizing price issues.

Offering to become involved early in the planning stages of a project and providing input that increases the value of the completed project and the client's profitability is more valuable today than being the low bidder. Going a step further and offering suggestions to maximize a client's investment in physical building requirements can be the determining factor that will set your company apart from any of your competitors.

The most successful A/E/C service marketers set themselves apart by first learning everything they possibly can about the client's business, goals, and planning process, and then applying this knowledge to help the client make the right decisions for his project requirements. Once a potential client recognizes that you can provide assistance based on a thorough knowledge of not just A/E/C services but of the client's specific industry as well, the client will likely respond by inviting you and other representatives of your company to join the planning process and eventually the implementation of the project. For example, you as a marketer might suggest that the client release a specialty building component early for manufacture to prevent delay in the overall schedule, thereby bringing the client's manufacturing process on line weeks or months earlier than anticipated, and thus increasing his/her profitability. In this manner, you make a measurable impact on the success of the project, a fact that you hope the client will not forget. This kind of service lives on in the minds of people with whom you do business, and is broadcast far and wide. *("You can count on Harry," he will say. "He's sure right on the spot when you need him.")* If you are able to do this, you have moved not only your client closer to success, but you and your firm as well.

Trusted Advisor

With this technique, you succeed in moving the discussion away from commodity pricing issues to one of recognition of professional services. You can also use your knowledge of the client's business and issues to sell pre-construction services to provide a competitive advantage for the construction phase.

Knowledge of the client also is critical for responding to a client's technical proposal requests. Rarely do clients give you sufficient information in proposal requests for A/E/C practitioners to recognize what is actually expected in proposals. Generally, the RFP is terse, with dry, technical language. It is simply a blueprint in words of what is essential to the project. If you go by the details of the RFP and reply in kind (which is what you must do), what you will end up with is a proposal that will be a duplicate of everyone else's proposal—directed specifically to the details of the RFP and not recognizing with a single word or effort what may be behind the RFP. By meeting with the prospective client early, you may be able to learn the client's expectations for the project. You may also be able, in casual conversation, to find out what he/she may be worried about: what concerns he or she might have concerning the project, what personal concerns he may have—and you will have a chance to respond more specifically to the RFP, taking into consideration the personal issues that he could not express in the dry, bureaucratic language generally used in an RFP. There lies your best chance of success: understanding that behind every RFP is a human being with human foibles, problems, concerns, and personal worries. Figure out how to help this person succeed, and you yourself will succeed.

If you are able to immerse yourself in each of the businesses of your prospective clients, you will be infinitely more effective in achieving success in your own goals than marketers who merely pass information along about their companies' capabilities.

This client-based knowledge is the reason that many larger A/E/C organizations separate their marketing programs by client industry type and arrange to have their marketers specialize in only a certain type of industry. This allows them to become more effective, both for the client and the

Client Focused, Market Driven

practitioner. For example, a construction firm might have some marketers targeting health care organizations, some targeting manufacturing corporations, and still others who specialize in commercial development. Specializing permits marketers to concentrate on one particular type of industry, enabling them to learn not only customer needs but general industry needs as well. This specialization enables marketers to become considerably more effective in helping their clients become successful, and ultimately the practitioner shares in this success. We are in the age of specialization; thus, if you become an "expert" in a particular field, everyone who needs this type of service will call upon you.

Although the manner of offering A/E/C services may have evolved somewhat, one thing never changes: the way a client should be treated. This basic principle must be incorporated into every marketing plan or initiative.

Chapter

2

Virtual Construction

A/E/C marketers must thoroughly familiarize themselves with how the business of architecture, engineering, construction, and related services is changing. These issues must be incorporated into marketing programs to assure clients, facing similar changes in their own industries, that the contractor is capable of meeting the challenges of the way business is being conducted today.

Virtual technology has become a reality in all industries, including design and construction. One clear example is found in the evolution of communications. From standard mail delivery, society has progressed to overnight express deliveries, facsimile transmissions, and now e-mail. If there is anywhere a faster and easier way to communicate, some bright young company will find it and put it on the market virtually overnight. Thus, if you are trying to put together a deal with someone across town, around the globe, or across the ocean, you can do it in hours or minutes, rather than days, weeks, or months.

Our Industry Today

Just a few decades ago, computer processing capability cost was measured in millions of dollars, processing time was measured in hours or days, storage required many cubic feet of space, and memory capacity was infinitesimal. Today, we have computers that cost less than $1,000 and processing time is measured in nanoseconds. The hard drive storage space of equipment that once occupied an entire floor of an office building is now contained in a few square inches of space. Memory capability in this space is now measured in gigabits, once unimaginable. Equally important, all these improvements come with quality that is unparalleled in any other industry.

For comparable improvements to have occurred in the A/E/C industry, an office building today would be designed and built in one minute, would cost pennies per square foot, and would have no defects or punch lists. The only problem with this comparison is that this office building would be about the size of a Monopoly game hotel and its useful life would be less than three years.

Customer requirements for speed and quality continue to increase. Those A/E/C firms that respond to these requirements will become increasingly successful, whereas those that do not will be left competing for smaller, marginally profitable niche markets. Real-time messaging has changed the way we do business. Do you still use a drawing board? A drafting pencil? A slide rule? We hardly think so.

Electronic Impact on A/E/C Services

There are several specific ways industry clients are changing the construction industry. For example, in real estate management, building owners have compressed the time required to upgrade existing tenant space—an important factor in maintaining a competitive edge in the rental market. By establishing strategic alliances with design firms and contractors and maintaining integrated databases of them, real estate consultants are able to relay information instantly among themselves to ensure that an owner's building receives the necessary upgrading and retrofitting as required. This process substantially lessens retrofit costs through early identification and streamlines the entire design and construction process.

In the same manner, through strategic alliances, design teams will soon be able to identify long-lead construction components early in the design phase and monitor the component's manufacture until contractual obligations of delivery are assumed by the contractor. Otis Elevators has already taken a major step forward in the virtual construction process. By providing a direct link to the manufacturer's information through the design team's computer-aided design (CAD) system, the designer is able to create an elevator system—customized to meet the owner's needs—well before it is actually manufactured.

The only way to make use of electronic capabilities is by complete electronic connectivity between all team members of the construction process—client, architect, engineer, contractor, subcontractors, and suppliers. Electronic capabilities alone do not sufficiently improve the overall processes of any industry unless all involved parties are connected to permit real-time communications and electronic management capabilities to improve the overall process or product. For example, the addition of CAD to the processes of an architectural firm does not by itself improve the overall construction process. The CAD capability only improves the architectural firm's design process internally and brings no significant improvement to the overall construction process, except that CAD compresses the time necessary to construct a plan, utilizing time more efficiently. For true electronic construction, the entire team, including the contractor and subcontractor, must be capable of using CAD drawings throughout all phases of the project.

Virtual construction is defined as the structuring of a corporation with complete electronic connectivity for each individual construction project; it involves the teaming of individual organizations required to complete the particular project. Virtual construction capability is centered on the client rather than being based upon the usual hierarchical organizational chart, allowing the client to interact with the entire team directly and instantly.

Virtual corporations, meaning the teams selected for a particular project, exist only as long as is necessary to complete a particular task. Upon completion of the task, the virtual corporation ceases to exist until another task is required and another team is assembled to complete it. Virtual corporations exist without physical space requirements, often operating only with computer connectivity linking employees together who might be located anywhere in the world. The people themselves occupy space, but the corporation concept depends on their assumed unity for the purposes of the current project. The entire far-flung group may be supervised by a single individual in a single cubicle with a single computer, or perhaps by a small group of people linked by computers directing the entire project.

Each virtual corporation is unique and consists only of the team members required for the task at hand. A virtual construction corporation is not the individual construction company as we have known it; it is the entire design and construction team assembled to complete one specific project for one specific client.

The concept of the virtual corporation has actually been applied in the construction field for decades, when a group of individual companies join together to design and build a single project for a specific client. The group of companies then disbands, moving forward to work on other projects. In the past, this has been known as "joint venturing."

Today, however, numerous paradigms have changed the way business is conducted in the design and construction profession. They require the entire building team to be connected electronically and to adapt and apply the computerization capabilities available to improve the overall quality, speed, and cost of every individual project.

Numerous industry clients, including the federal government, have long ago moved to virtual construction. OSHA's "negotiated rule making" is computerized and links all negotiating parties electronically. This facilitates the immediate review of process rule changes and waivers, eliminating the need for endless paperwork, redundant and time-consuming meetings, and unnecessary costs. The Chesapeake Division of the U.S. Navy has for years required that all as-built drawings be computerized and stored on CD-ROMs, eliminating mountains of blueprint rolls. The Department of the Army also has instituted the "paperless acquisition vision" in order to eliminate paper.

So, of course, we in the design and construction business have followed suit. Nothing takes up less space than a CD! If you haven't done so yet, it makes sense to explore this option.

The age of technology

A lifetime of documented information for people in the 16th century would today be contained in less than one week's worth of the average daily newspaper. The rate at which employees are exposed to information continues to grow faster each year largely due to the capability of computers to process information at continually faster rates.

It is no longer acceptable to take three to seven years from design through construction to complete a typical building project. As the industry's clients move to respond to their customers' requirements of instant production, so too must the construction industry respond to its clients.

External changes

Corporations now place an increased emphasis on *infostructure* rather than infrastructure. Physical highways are less important to an organization's success than the information highway. Whenever possible, companies are eliminating physical assets. For example, in communities across the country, telecommuting is becoming as common as commuting to an office for work.

The number of employees working from home or other distant locations continues to increase yearly, and now is measured in tens of millions of people. Not only do employees telecommute to work by connecting with their office from home, but other concepts of the virtual office affect the industry as well. These include the concept of "hoteling," which provides temporary physical office space at a company's location to employees on a shared basis. Rather than providing one office for one employee, corporations now can combine the use of telecommuting and hoteling, giving employees access to a physical office or conference room on an as-needed basis. Numerous other employees share this space, thus the term *hoteling*.

The federal government also embraces the electronic age by establishing telecommuting centers in remote suburban locations to allow employees to work closer to home using virtual technology. This eliminates long commutes for thousands of federal employees, particularly near Washington, DC, and assists the government in meeting increased EPA clean air standards less expensively than by other means. Computerization of more and more business processes influences the shelter needs of many companies. For example, legal firms no longer allocate valuable space to house hard-copy law book collections. Legal research is now completed using computers. In addition, most lawyers now use personal computers, limiting the need for clerical staff. The same can be said for many other professions, including design and engineering. In fact, technology has effectively reduced physical office space requirements of corporations by tens of millions of square feet for the next decade.

This concept permits locating an employee directly in a client's office until a specific assignment is completed. The advantage of having the employee work literally next to the client optimizes meeting the requirements of the specific project, with better and faster results. This capability has actually taken partnering to higher levels; one virtual organization is formed until the specific project is completed. Numerous engineering and construction firms have taken advantage of this concept, working through the early planning and design stages directly with the client to facilitate the faster completion of the building project and to increase overall quality and customer satisfaction.

An example of the use of this *virtual office concept* is the completion by J. A. Jones Construction Company, Charlotte, NC, and Benham Group, Oklahoma City, OK, of an Ocean Spray juice syrup facility in Nevada. To meet the schedule demands of completing the manufacturing facility in record time from concept to production, Jones and Benham placed their key project personnel in Ocean Spray's offices to facilitate the planning, design, and construction of the project. From concept to production, the team partnered directly with the client to complete the project in severely curtailed time parameters and to meet the goals of designing and installing new food processes based on the owner's product requirements.

The concept of virtual offices has directly affected the construction industry by requiring less and less physical office space, particularly in city centers. No longer is it necessary for an organization to have a high-rise headquarters building in a downtown location to be "noticed." In the electronic age, it is more productive to be noticed on the Internet than on a city street.

It is evident that high-rise construction in metropolitan centers, although not extinct, has been curtailed compared to the 1980s. Companies realize that it is no longer practical to require employees to commute to a central location, preferring instead to bring the work to the employees by providing suburban locations for their physical office needs. This closely parallels the telecommuting and virtual office space paradigms, creating again a direct external impact on the construction industry by changing clients' needs for office space.

Although we have seen vast improvements in technological capabilities over the past 25 years, the next 25 years will be spent learning to take advantage of and implementing these capabilities within the industry. In much the same manner that VCR manufacturers have made their product easier to program, technology firms are managing the process to bring their products into mainstream usage.

Many design firms are making effective use of design programs that use animated three-dimensional geometry from CAD files to enable clients to inspect proposed designs before construction begins. This computerized walk-through lets architects apply various colors, textures, and material finishes to proposed designs to determine what is the optimal scheme for the client.

CAD drawings and specifications will become fully integrated into project management controls. Contractors will be able to use virtual reality software to work with the project schedule rather than rely on critical path programs. CAD files also will enable contractors to determine a perfectly accurate quantity of materials to better estimate and control project costs. Smart or expert software will be incorporated into the project management controls that automatically direct the computer to check for inconsistencies in designs, including conflicts between the architectural and structural or mechanical drawings.

These improvements will all be used not only to increase the industry's overall product quality but also to compress project schedules to meet the growing demand for instant satisfaction.

No longer can a computer chip manufacturer wait three to seven years for a facility to produce a computer chip that has a useful life of less than one year. The external improvements will be used to compress the overall schedule of a typical project, including planning, design, and construction, to less than one year. It will become mainstream only if more aggressive construction firms establish this goal as their standard.

Internal improvements

Although much of the influence during the next decade will come externally, many advances in construction products and services will come from within the industry. Material improvements that offer better quality and price continue to evolve. Metals will become less important in construction because plastics are increasingly being used for structural components. Plastic composite beams are now replacing steel in some designs. Plastic piping for plumbing is increasingly being included in building codes.

Improved concrete mixes now include self-healing concrete, which has the ability to close small fissures and cracks that often appear in the finished product. Concrete with limited flexural strength is also being tested for commercial use. The potential of such flexibility is endless. Paint with the ability to clean itself of mildew, stains, and even graffiti is now available. Such products will become more prevalent on the market as construction material manufacturers adapt the use of computer modeling and testing to improve their product lines.

In conjunction with these new products, typical construction products are becoming "smart"—i.e., able to adapt to changing external conditions as necessary. For example, glass used in certain walls will darken itself during the sunny portion of the day and then become lighter to allow additional sunlight to pass through during other periods of time. Exterior wall components will be able to monitor unsuitable conditions, alerting the building engineer of conditions such as excess moisture that might be evidence of leaks. Flooring may contain sensors to adjust the climate and lighting controls in an individual room when foot traffic enters.

Subcontractors' roles

Operating in the virtual world precludes any organization from operating in a vacuum isolated from both suppliers and customers, and this has become increasingly true in the design and construction industry. To meet the demands of virtual scheduling and instant gratification of the industry's clients, contractors must respond by becoming connected with all team members and, in particular, with subcontractors and trade contractors.

Few contractors today are true general contractors, performing all the work on a project themselves; rather, they perform as construction managers and subcontract the majority of the work on a project. Subcontractors have become the niche experts within the industry, providing the technological knowledge of a specific building trade. This knowledge must be incorporated into the early phases of project planning and design to meet the demands of the industry's clients for faster and better delivery of the construction project.

As technical experts in their specific niche markets, subcontractors can directly assist design firms in selecting products and components that enhance the overall design by making pertinent suggestions about what can be done to reduce construction schedules and costs while improving the overall quality of the finished product. The participation of subcontractors in early planning is even more critical for design-build contracting.

Design-build contracting

Design-build contracting can trace its beginnings back to the master builders of the Egyptian pyramids. Some 4,000 years ago, the master builder completed both the design and construction and performed all field activities. Under this contracting method, there was clearly one single point of responsibility—the master builder. In the past few decades, the design and construction industry has moved away from design-build and self-performed work, not because of problems with the method, but in order to transfer legal liability to other entities as the legal profession became entrenched within the industry.

Architects and engineers, by using the low-bid separate construction contract, would transfer the design obligations to the owner, who must indemnify the general contractor for design errors under the contract. Contractors, in turn, subcontract most, if not all, of the work in order to pass the liability on to subcontractors and suppliers. In the past few decades, as there has been an increase in this system of transferring the liability, design plans required specifications separate from the drawings, not necessarily for the purpose of improving the quality of the finished product, but to pass the liability from designer to contractor, and then allow the contractor to pass this liability on to subcontractors. Plans of decades ago were limited, with all written documentation appearing directly on the plans. The voluminous plans and specifications required today (not to mention written contracts) to complete even the simplest project have resulted in projects becoming bogged down by disputes and extended completion schedules.

Industry clients have responded by turning back the clock to the proven methods of design-build, which places all liability on a single source, and improves delivery schedules considerably. The increasing demands for faster and faster delivery of the construction product will certainly nudge the industry toward wider acceptance of the design-build method of contracting. Although the requirement to use design-build is an external preference, it may become the contracting and design method preferred by progressive firms that implement programs to respond to the need for instant satisfaction.

Direct computerized linkage

All project participants will electronically link together to share the project's information database to improve the overall quality, cost, and schedule of individual construction projects. Each project team becomes a virtual corporation, coming together to complete a project, then disbanding to form virtual corporations for other projects. Linkage is established in the conceptual stages of a project when subcontractors can participate to improve the design process that leads to improvements in the construction phase.

CAD files will become the nucleus of the virtual construction organization. All planning, design, purchasing, scheduling, and communications will grow from the project's CAD files. Estimates in the planning stages will be updated as the design progresses or is changed, with quantities of materials being automatically adjusted. This enables contractors to provide the client with a constantly updated project cost through the design phase, in order to better control costs in the construction phase.

Smart software also permits self-monitoring of designs to detect any mechanical or structural mistakes or inconsistencies between the various trades. This software also verifies building code compliance.

Contractors and subcontractors will use these CAD files to institute early release and ordering of long lead-time items identified by the computer and use the program to monitor the production of these items.

Files and correspondence among team members will be transmitted instantly, with each team member aware of all actions that may affect progress during the construction phase. However, this communication linkage is effective only if project management is structured linearly; it eliminates the hierarchical organization common in construction today.

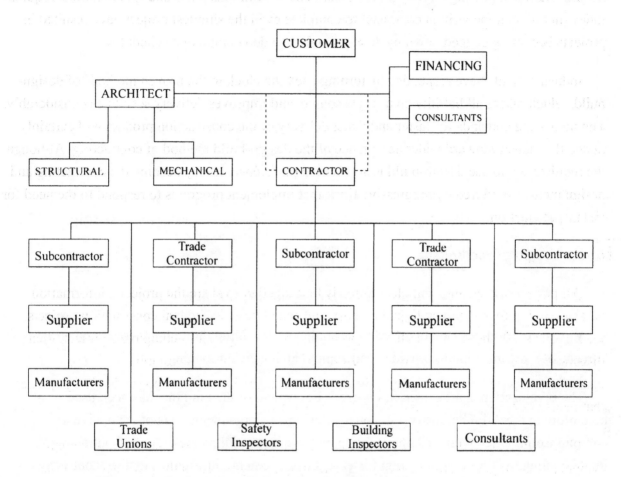

Figure 2.1. Typical organization chart implemented by general contractors.

Linear project organization

In every virtual corporation, a linear organization is structured to utilize the closest and fastest line of direct communication between the client and the employee responsible for the work.

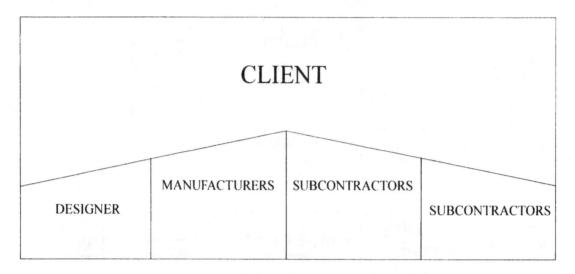

Figure 2.2. Linear organizational chart.

Virtual corporations cannot afford to have clients struggling through a hierarchical and bureaucratic organization to provide needed input and decision-making.

The organization chart shown in **Figure 2.1** is typical of the kind that has been used heretofore in the A/E/C industry. Obviously, this type of organization is not conducive to communicating effectively or implementing electronic scheduling techniques. Contractors implementing the linear organization for virtual management must realize that subcontractors need direct links to the client, and the contractor must also be directly linked to the subcontractors' suppliers. The ultimate purpose of a virtual organization is to permit instant communication, which eliminates any form of hierarchical organization, such as that shown in **Figure 2.2.**

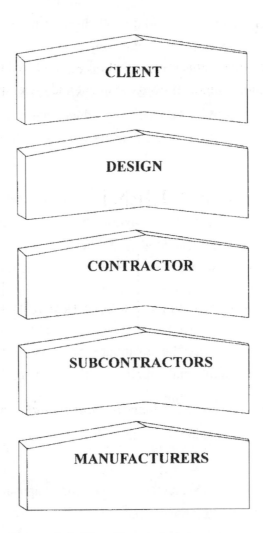

Figure 2.3. Top-down management.

In a linear virtual organization, the subcontractor will have considerably more input in the overall project success. The top-down management style (as shown in **Figure 2.3**), created from the need to pass liability down to lower-tier subcontractors, is not effective in a linear organization. The virtual A/E/C organization must implement the upside-down contracting method of managing to be successful in the future.

Intensive and early subcontractor involvement

Although relatively ignored in construction, manufacturing and service sector industries have literally been turning themselves upside down and inside out in the revolution of reorganizing corporate structures to compete in the electronic age. Changes in management philosophy occur based on an integration with suppliers that encourages extensive outsourcing to improve overall quality and competitiveness.

At its foundation, this revolution is based on changing from intra-organization (within one company) to inter-organization (among several companies) management, which promotes strategic linking with suppliers, subcontractors, and consultants. This networking affords immediate links with talented people throughout the world, referred to as "just in time" talent. Far-flung corporations often provide services or products that are superior in quality, quickly produced, and less expensive because of their teaming relationships with suppliers and subcontractors.

Suppliers, now an integral part of many manufacturing industries, are included in the process from conceptual design to quality controls. Manufacturers select team members not on price issues alone, but also on networking capability and performance abilities. Supplier relationships have become so crucial that manufacturers' employee performance reviews now include evaluations of the employee's ability to deal effectively with suppliers.

The interaction of these relationships will change as the industry's clients and progressive designers and contractors realize that the advantages of inter-organizational processes are essential to success. Subcontractors and suppliers will become closely linked with contractors and design teams, forming strategic alliances to change the direction of the industry.

The benefits of upside-down contracting that place a greater dependency on subcontractors include:

- cost reductions from subcontractors' input during design and pre-construction services
- faster response time to innovations
- superior quality improvements
- compression of project schedules
- improved communications
- greater profitability
- improved networking and alliances

Information that is driven from the bottom up will make contracting more successful through positive relationships and interdependency with suppliers and subcontractors.

Whereas client concerns previously focused on the time value of money, they are now concentrated on the money value of time. Clients whose own industries are facing the information age successfully demand that the construction industry make maximum use of electronic communications in order to make the most of time value. This process is being achieved in other industries by direct networking with suppliers and subcontractors, allowing this immediate information processing to achieve the time value standards necessary in order to be competitive.

Pre-construction services may become key to a project's overall success, as contractors offer connectivity and access to a virtual team, including upside-down management, during the conceptual phases of a project. Contractors form strategic alliances with clients to provide project management by processing information throughout the project. Team members who participate in a project may, in fact, never actually be part of the physical construction, offering their services only through electronics. The construction industry faces numerous new paradigms, and those firms that step outside their "boxes" and create new services will become the industry leaders.

Time compression

The increasing need to compress schedule parameters of a typical building project forces the design and construction industry to implement techniques to reduce the time needed to produce a completed project. Critical path method (CPM) scheduling by itself is no longer capable of meeting these scheduling demands. The industry has begun to implement virtual scheduling techniques.

In construction, as the time value of money grows, there is an increasing dependency upon effective computerized scheduling software. In a move to virtual scheduling, major construction organizations now tie their priority scheduling programs directly into their subcontractors' and suppliers' production control systems. A contractor can then receive a continuous stream of data directly from the supplier's production line. By constantly tracking the component's manufacture, the contractor can integrate product-specific information directly into the overall project schedule to accurately reflect the component's actual delivery and installation date.

This eliminates costly trips to the supplier's production facility to physically verify production schedules. Should production problems arise, this tracking technique makes it much easier to develop an alternative action plan, if necessary, to keep the project on schedule. The increased use of virtual scheduling will have a tremendous impact on project delivery, resulting in a faster, improved construction process for the entire industry.

Virtual scheduling demands that all participants on a project be electronically connected to provide instant communications, improve building scheduling, and meet the requirements of the project. Combining CAD files, critical path methods, and other project files into a communications database shared by all members of the project team should be standard in the industry.

For example, computerized schedules will be instantly updated to track the production of precast panels at the factory, piece by piece. Smart software now available will update the schedule, alerting team members to required changes and preventing slippage of the schedule.

This same software will enable subcontractors who have early start dates to be automatically informed if material is shipped earlier than originally scheduled. Electronic schedules will not be I-J node charts that hang on job trailer walls that no one ever looks at. Electronic schedules will be totally interactive and continually updated. With such schedules, the team can *manage* the project rather than react after it is too late to implement the necessary steps to maintain the schedule.

Tomorrow's A/E/C Industry

What will tomorrow's job site look like? It will most certainly be paperless. All drawings, schedules, requisitions, transmittals, and other "paperwork" will be on the computer and linked electronically through wireless transmission so the entire project team can have access to all information on the job, regardless of anyone's physical location.

The two major technological trends changing the industry are electronic data integration (EDI) and wireless communications. EDI allows the user to integrate several previously incompatible software programs to perform complex functions in unison. For example, by integrating a word processing software program with CAD drawing files and estimating software, the computer can be used to create a quantity total of every nut and bolt of the design. This will make the estimating function, subject to inaccuracy due to human error, totally accurate and completed in seconds rather than days or weeks. This technology could shift the function of estimating from the contractor to the architect.

Software such as ProjecTrak, a leading Lotus Notes and Internet suite of business software, is another example of technology that is available. The program enables the creation of a common database. It can be established on a desktop computer and linked to all project team members. The software incorporates all data created during a project including CAD files, specifications, correspondence, schedules, shop drawings, spreadsheets, and other electronic data. Lotus Notes creates the database that permits team members to search the records for a specific item, including the entire history of documentation related to that specific item. This brings partnering to a new level, allowing all team members to access and share pertinent information. At the completion of the project, the contractor can turn over the CD-ROMs that contain the entire historical documentation, including as-built drawings.

Improvement in wireless communication also accelerates access to information directly in fieldwork activities. Handheld wireless computers and eyeglass monitors are already standard tools for superintendents. At the construction job site of the future, the superintendent on the tenth floor of the structure can review the placement of concrete. The superintendent accesses the CAD drawings for a related reinforcing detail and transmits a clarification memo to the engineer, who in turn transmits back to the job site the revised detail, and simultaneously updates the project's records.

This communications technology requires a complete disregard for hierarchical organization charts on the project. As in the case above, the superintendent is able to communicate directly with the structural engineer without having to submit the request to the contractor's office and then to the architect, who can then relay it to the engineer. When the question is answered, this archaic process would have to be repeated in the reverse order. Such outdated communications channels will be abandoned in the future to permit the transmission of information to take place instantly. No longer will each person in the process need to wait until information has been passed down the line. Employees at all levels of an organization must share the responsibility for processing information to eliminate the red tape that in the past used to slow the process to a crawl.

These internal and external changes will create a radically different A/E/C industry in the next few decades, consolidating five key virtual management techniques: (1) direct computerized linkage; (2) linear project organization; (3) intensive and early subcontractor involvement; (4) time compression of design and construction schedules; and (5) emphasis on information processing to increase profitability.

Chapter

3

How Business is

Done Today

The architecture of the building industry has not changed in more than 50 decades. For the last century, the overriding premise in the A/E/C industry was to keep your head down and keep working. This is actually a comfortable manner of doing work because you simply concentrate on the task at hand and give minimal thought to the environmental dynamics around you. If you were an estimator, you completed your estimate and turned it in to the sales or management department, which in turn bundled it into a neat package and forwarded it on to the bid authority. Individuals within companies usually did not concern themselves with what was happening among other comparable companies. There was security in their jobs as long as they kept doing the task at hand.

Then came the 1990s, and the rules we were all familiar with disappeared as companies and individuals fought to survive in a new world order. Money supplies dwindled, downsizing became the norm, new projects became scarce or nonexistent, few jobs were available within the industry (as well as elsewhere), workforce problems became much more prevalent and more complex, productivity dropped to a new low, costs kept rising, and margins became increasingly tighter. As companies tightened their belts and the marketplace was flooded with "consultants," the boom America had experienced in the '80s became the doom of the '90s. No longer was there any kind of security. Whereas the industry had been crying for workers in the '80s, in the '90s, 12 million individuals left a construction industry that prior to this time had demanded an annual increase of 200,000 new workers. In addition, the workforce that was left in place after the downturn had the lowest skill level in construction in more than 40 years, with only 27 percent of workers meeting the skills needed in the trades. Across the country, a reduction in available technical educational options reduced further the availability of talent needed. The national labor unions and schools remained unable to meet the severe challenges felt by the building industry. For companies to obtain work, their owners had to get out in the arena and make things happen. They tried everything they could think of because they didn't know which of the options would generate an order for the company. On top of that, a sort of musical chairs exercise took place in which many people were suddenly thrust out of the comfortable niche in which they had spent the previous 20 years and found they had to fend for themselves with a new employer, new methods of doing work, and the knowledge that the security they had previously enjoyed was gone forever.

The industry that emerged from this dynamic reorganization was faced with a complete restructuring of its culture. New external pressures were felt. The industry was realigning itself. The environment vibrated with new buzzwords. There was talk of design build, construction management, build-to-suit. Those still in the workforce had to take on new roles. Jobs that had been vacated were simply loaded on the shoulders of those who remained. The concept of total quality management was bandied about and resulted in the inclusion of many value-added activities and services in the overall building process. This required even more services on top of a compressed margin structure. Workers became increasingly stressed as the workload became greater yet. Partnering was not only discussed but actually implemented on many job sites around the country.

Technology became a driving force within the building industry as a method of improving productivity, given the reduction in staffing. These new technologies altered the landscape of design and construction. Suddenly architects were able to provide 3-D CAD simulation and visualization to express their ideas and concepts. This cross-disciplinary approach created new ideas about how business should be conducted and provided initial training to individuals who had never ventured across this unknown turf before.

Culture changes continued as sustainable materials, protection of the environment, and globalization altered the way we viewed our world.

With all these changes, it was apparent that the industry had to move in a new direction. The U.S. economy depends on new construction. Those of us facing the challenges—understanding that the economy consistently fluctuates, and what is down today must be up tomorrow—realized that we needed to overcome the recession of the '90s and prepare for the decade to come.

It is an exciting time to be in the industry and experience the radical change in a culture that has not experienced change for decades. It may be disturbing, but the outcome will position America and the industry far into the future. Three enormous tasks need to be done:

1. Break down destructive industry paradigms within the different segments of the A/E/C community
2. Overcome the extremely poor image within the industry that has created a shortage of workers
3. Continue to foster a culture within the industry of innovation and creativity

What Innovative Companies are Doing to Prepare for the Future

An article in *Architectural Record* entitled "Lessons from America's Best Managed Firms" made the comment that "in the 1990's the firms with the best numbers are often the ones that pay their associates well, offer generous benefits packages, and give to their community." This should not be surprising. While a jobseeker's primary incentive is a good salary and benefits, there's more to the average job than just money. People want to work for a good company. Most people in the industry spend more time in the office working with business associates than they do at home with their families. Is it any wonder, then, that they want this environment to be stimulating, challenging, and rewarding—and perhaps even inspiring?

Good management makes good sense today. We have seen a wealth of new management "systems" sweeping the industry: total quality management, best practices, entrepreneurial companies, partnering/collaborative management, chaos management, fast track, client-driven and value-added systems, benchmarking, and empowerment. Business styles will come and go; buzzwords flash in the business arena and fizzle out in weeks; but the revolution taking place in the marketplace—flextime, telecommuting, part time, new employee attitudes and demands—has restructured the business environment, and controls what successful companies are doing today.

The following examples show what several major construction and design companies are doing to prepare to meet the future head-on. Many are trying some of the popular buzzwords within their marketing and business plans. Some ideas, obviously, will work, and others will need to be adjusted to meet the realities of a company's individual markets and economies.

M. A. Mortenson, Minneapolis, MN, a leading construction company involved in the development, engineering, and construction of wind power projects throughout the United States, has an impressive resume. Since 1998, the company has been involved in the construction of 14 wind projects. However, it also is involved in aviation, education, health care and sports facilities, as well as power plants, dams, and many other types of projects. Projects include FedEx Forum, a new arena for the NBA's Memphis Grizzlies, and the Walt Disney Concert Hall, the new home for the Los Angeles Philharmonic Orchestra. Mortenson has been in business since 1954. This company, as an example, is working hard to integrate the delivery of design and construction services to facilitate this new market reality. It has developed each department within the company to be technology driven, it has expanded its services, and it requires continual education of all members of its teams. Besides this, it has established a proliferation of strategic alliances with current and potential partners for future opportunities as they arise.

An article in *Contractor* magazine discussed how contractors could market their companies in the "century of the consumer." It mentioned that the 130 contractors in attendance at a marketing meeting agreed that contractors must differentiate to survive. The industry has emerged from a recession in the early nineties, and the best of the best have survived and are battling for control of every dollar remaining in the market. All these contractors have similar costs, margins, and quality; the winning contractors are the ones who have differentiated themselves in the details.

So how do you differentiate and concentrate on perfecting the details? The *Contractor* article spoke of a customer who had a problem with his septic tank on a hot Saturday in the summer. He called the septic tank contractor, who immediately sent over a plumber, who arrived wearing a wet suit, who fixed the problem before a group of guests were due to arrive. Whom do you suppose the customer called the next time he had a plumbing project? Some might consider a

Saturday service call to be beyond the call of duty. However, it is the unique approach that nets the next project. Most companies do what is required to produce quality work today; successful companies put forth additional effort, in order to stay ahead of the competition.

New forces in the marketplace demand that companies become much more innovative. Customers today require flexibility, and firms must employ an expanding arsenal of new technological tools to be effective in designing and constructing buildings. Customers and clients have become much more sophisticated in their approach to the building industry process, in large part because of the shortening of product delivery times, which creates further pressure to improve delivery and construction services. Not only must buildings be built more quickly, but also builders need to incorporate advanced technologies that will affect end users of these structures as well as life-cycle costs for maintenance, operations, and even potential reuse and sale.

One such sophisticated client is Microsoft Corporation, which puts projects on a fast track at its Redmond, WA, campus. With delivery times for computer products having accelerated, owners of the buildings intended to house such products must get their new structures up, running, and producing as soon as possible...before the products to be sold within the structure have reached the end of *their* life span. Twelve months for a completion date is not unheard of for a $100 million high-tech project.

Technology has even changed our paradigm of what comprises an office building. The concept of *hoteling* in the office environment has affected the trend toward more and more telecommuting and job sharing. Office workers have their "offices" on carts that contain a computer, desktop accessories, and files. Workers check the carts out on the days they are in the office and set up a virtual office within whatever space is convenient. Otherwise, they work on laptop computers with cell phones and fax machines at home or even while traveling.

Hilti North America, Tulsa, OK, is a global leader in products and systems for fastening, demolition, positioning, fire-stop, and construction. It primarily sells equipment and power tools. Its 2,000 employees live and work in hundreds of communities from coast to coast.

Hilti operates with its workforce in mobile vans. Local sales representatives, on an as-needed basis, can use a location that has a showroom, a service center, and a small bank of offices. But generally, workers have everything they need with them in the van. This is simplified even further by having its principal telephone number at headquarters in Oklahoma, from which the operator pages a local representative to respond to calls. Most clients have no idea that this company maintains a "virtual" corporation, managed from a national headquarters thousands of miles away from local offices.

This is an example of how many corporations manage customer service. If you have a maintenance contract for your home appliances with any major company, its toll-free number will get you to a local representative, even though your call may have initially reached an operator a thousand miles away.

Ceco Concrete Construction is considered the nation's largest formwork subcontractor. Operating in a centralized location in Kansas City, MO, the company works with other branches of its parent firm and subcontracts to other firms to complete sizable projects. At that location, safety, contract management, accounting, human resources, and payroll are handled for the various satellite business units. These business units are further refined around regional hubs, which are broken down into smaller strategic business units with anywhere from one to five members on staff.

One large project managed by Ceco was the expansion of Dulles International Airport in Chantilly, VA. Ceco acted as a subcontractor to M. A. Mortenson using the above concept of reduced staffing, dispersed personnel, and technological advancement. The organizational structure they used is shown in **Figure 3.1.**

Drawings produced by Skidmore, Owings & Merrill in its Washington, DC, office were provided electronically for Mortenson, which sent the plans to various suppliers and subcontractors. Ceco, for example, downloaded the drawings to an AutoCAD detailer in Detroit, MI. When the detailer completed the necessary work, the drawings were downloaded to an engineer in Atlanta, GA. He reviewed the details, made modifications, and downloaded his details to a print shop in Chantilly and to the project manager at the job site at Dulles. The project manager, in turn, checked the drawings and gave Mortenson a hard copy and a disk overlay for the project. As project changes evolved, this same procedure took place on a daily basis, and a finished product usually could be presented to the contractor and the architect later that same day. Pricing of the changes was accomplished locally by the project manager.

Weekly payrolls were sent electronically to the central Kansas City office, prepared there, and expressed back to the job site the next day. Most communication was done electronically and documented accordingly. An electronic link to more than 20 other office locations assisted the project manager in finding solutions to the problems encountered. Usually someone else in the organization had experienced the same problem in the past.

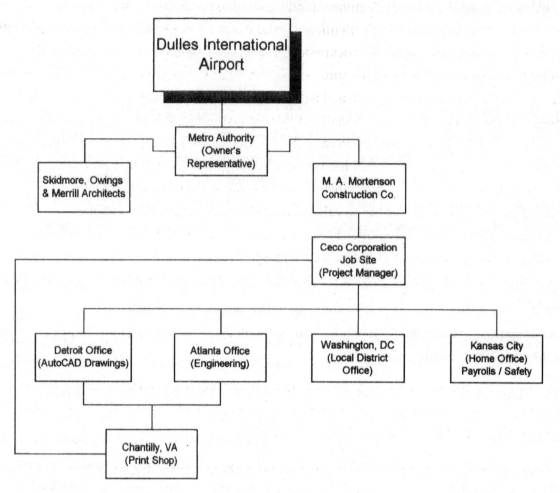

Figure 3.1. Virtual construction site with reach across the United States.

This large and complex project was essentially managed by a single project manager and one superintendent, who worked in concert to meet the needs of the project and do it as efficiently and quickly as possible. Ceco worked with a small core of executives and full-time employees, and assigned much of the group's fluctuating work volume to outside contractors, part-time help, and consultants.

Like Ceco, Turner Construction Company has established a series of core offices around the country with a strong client focus. Based in Dallas, TX, with offices throughout the United States, Turner has consistently been in the forefront of the national construction arena due to its ability to be flexible in industry needs and trends. The company has established a reputation for building top-quality projects on time and within budget, but it takes this process one step further by developing partnerships that potentially can last a lifetime, according to Turner's Tom Paci. The office that develops a relationship follows the client wherever it goes. This customer alliance has allowed Turner to lead the country in sales revenue for a number of years in selected market segments.

NAVFAC (Naval Facilities Administration), under the leadership of Rear Admiral David Nash, has been transformed from a traditional government agency to a 21st-century organization. Nash has ushered in new forms of procurement, such as design-build, and has enhanced NAVFAC's ongoing partnering programs, and is minimizing past problems with litigation. His spirit and enthusiasm are contagious, and he has instilled a team feeling in the construction divisions of the agency. What is especially of interest here is that this new spirit has spawned public/private ventures with the opportunity for civilian ownership. The culture of innovation and enthusiasm engendered by Nash has spread to other governmental divisions as his agency interacts with them. Captain Julian Sabatini, with the Naval Construction Division in Washington, DC, states that he has developed a much closer partnership with the design/construction community. NAVFAC puts an emphasis on best-value procurement methods, including design-build and negotiated projects that attract a qualified base of builders to work with in the future. This innovative segment of the government has led the way for other agencies.

Rand Construction Engineering, Inc., of Brighton, MI, is a multifaceted firm. From banks to universities, automobile manufacturers to car dealerships, and railroads to waste management, the company offers a variety of services, including construction administration, site selection, soil testing, environmental analysis, and handling of governmental approvals and permits. This 20-year-old firm has distinguished itself in the industry.

Rand Construction was originally a minority business enterprise that has grown tenfold. The construction industry traditionally has had strong perceptions of how work should be done, formerly focusing on sheer brawn. The current Rand leadership has led the company by utilizing the newest techniques, such as networking. Its leaders learned early on that clients want a construction company that can provide a new facility as fast as possible, with the highest quality and at the least cost.

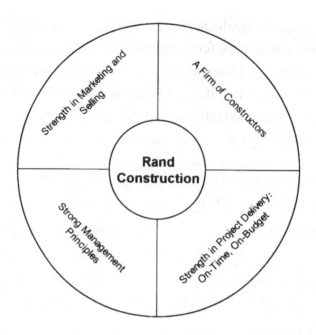

Figure 3.2. Rand Construction's model for success.

The constant development of relationships and the leaders challenging their teams to develop innovative construction methods based on best practices has allowed Rand to grow. The company attributes most of its success to flexibility and dedication to quality. This flexibility has meant the ability to do all types of projects—from very small to large—effectively, on time, and profitably. Rand never stops searching the market for new opportunities, in order to maintain a continuous flow of work and consistently increase market share (see **Figure 3.2**).

TDX Construction Corporation is a construction management company based in Manhattan that focuses on interiors, education, health facilities, and laboratories, and is doing the very best it can to service them. TDX has achieved success by developing a close relationship with a key segment of the construction community, the New York Dormitory Authority. One of the firm's partners, Logan Hurst, has stated that TDX's reputation for quality and performance has been gained slowly but steadily. TDX utilizes the latest technology in many aspects of the construction process, including estimating, project management coordination, cost control, scheduling, and project documentation. Relationships are the driving force for the company, and mandate close ties with client representatives in a tight, competitive market. TDX's practice of hiring the best possible people, providing ongoing training, and establishing a culture of developing new business opportunities has been an integral element of the firm's philosophy.

Symmons Industries, based in Braintree, MA, is a manufacturer of residential and commercial building products, primarily plumbing products. The company guarantees its products for the life of the home in which they are installed for as long as the original owner lives there. In advertising, Kevin Symmons, former president, used to illustrate this concept by standing in a white bathrobe with a hammer and chisel in hand in front of a stone monolith engraved with the inscription "Built to last 1,000 years." A guarantee is difficult to provide, but if a company is truly serious about quality and service, this strategy can create an invaluable market niche.

As you can see from these various examples, the attitudes, practices, and beliefs of these companies have been structured to meet the realities of today's market economy. They can't be overlooked as being insignificant.

Rick Dutmer, a director for FMI, management consultants to the construction industry, has stated that companies that experience long-term profitability have a culture of positive attitudes. These attitudes allow employees to understand the relationship among profits, benefits, and salaries. This attitude factor is the key aspect of any business and even more relevant in the competitive market we are faced with today.

You Control Your Future and the Future of Your Company

We all have the ability to influence our future through the actions we take to accomplish the goals and visions we set for our companies and ourselves. We don't always recognize this influence, but it can have a considerable impact on the outcome we desire. Let's look at a few examples of how individuals influence outcome or perception.

Authority

To lead change within your organization, you must be able to differentiate the authority and influence you have from the actions you take. We have all heard of the Peter Principle, which says that you rise to your level of incompetence. When you are first promoted to oversee a group of employees, initially you manage this group through your authority. But as an individual rises in the corporation, he or she is not able to physically oversee what each of these individuals does and must rely more and more on influence to sway their thoughts and actions. When you discover that you have taken on more and more personally and feel you are losing control of the results, you begin to experience the variance between the authority given to you and your influence over the outcome of these activities.

Influence

Cold calls are another good example of how each of us uses influence in a situation where we lack authority. You walk into a potential client's office, introduce yourself to the client, and discuss your services and the benefits that your firm can bring to that company. You are not always successful, but you are exerting influence on the situation through your direct actions.

We all see individuals each day who flex their authority but wield no influence. When this action fails to achieve desired results, managers become more authoritarian and strive to push more. But without personal influence, little can be achieved.

An individual we worked with in the past consistently missed deadlines. He knew the time required to complete estimates but never seemed to be able to meet the dates set by the office manager to have his estimate completed and ready for review by the office and field staff for a bid. Many times the project would be bid from a marginally reviewed estimate because there was no time left for a thorough review. He was consistently told that he was missing deadlines. But being told did little to change his behavior. Another approach would have been to sit down with him and let him set the date for the staff meeting, in a time frame that would be conducive to total staff review. Then he is involved in the decision-making process and can take responsibility for his own actions. He would then have an open-door policy to discuss assembling the bid and what it would take to make sure the bid is available by the date that was established by him.

The result is that his supervisor would influence this individual's actions by allowing him to assume responsibility for his own assignment, and he would then receive the credit for bringing the estimate in on the date he established, not one set arbitrarily by the office manager. From this example, we're sure you can recognize examples of situations that probably happen in your shop, where perhaps you can affect the outcome through your personal influence.

As the above examples suggest, each of us has the ability to influence others, but we don't necessarily use it to its full impact, just as we fail to use our brains or bodies to their full capacity. An increase of 5 to 10 percent of your personal influence would have a considerable impact on your productivity, success rate, and satisfaction.

Your future leadership ability is limited only by your inability to take action to solve each dilemma that you face. Tackling each impossible task one by one by use of your personal influence can greatly maximize the results you achieve. Achieving what others cannot is the way to differentiate yourself within your company and with your clients.

You lead and influence others daily through your words and deeds. You control what others do through your actions and how you attempt to solve the problems you encounter. This is a constant in all of our lives. You must take responsibility for the results of the tasks for which you are responsible because it is your influence that will mark the final result. You are in control of the future for your personal success and for the success of your company. If the company is not headed in the right direction, it is up to you to assist with its redirection. This allows you to manage the climate within an organization.

Jim Clark is CEO of the Clark Construction Group, a provider of construction services that was established 1906 and is headquartered in Bethesda, MD. He is known for his dedication to getting the very best prices from subcontractors to ensure the lowest possible price and the greatest likelihood of success on bid day. He does this by being present every time his team is working on a bid, speaking with each person involved in assembling the numbers, and then stressing how important success is for the entire organization and the families of every employee of the company. The effort being made is not just an ordinary bid, but the way in which each employee can help himself as well as fellow workers and continue to ensure the success of the company.

The last factor of influence is the leverage attainable from commitment—not only from company officers but also from project managers and all employees from top to bottom. The dynamics of today's business mandate that all employees provide constant commitment to the outcome of each project. Each person in the building industry today wears many hats, and each is just as important as the next. Because of overlapping activities, jobs, and projects, a domino effect is the result when any one individual does not do his or her job properly. It is critical to ensure total commitment from everyone involved. You can ensure this by inspiring their commitment to the assignments they handle. Your influence on their actions to achieve positive results can make a significant difference to the entire company.

Commitment necessary to sink or swim

None of us really likes commitment. When a spouse asks if his or her mate will promise to be home on time on a particular evening, the mate might think, "Sure, I want to be here. But anything can happen on the job."

This example certainly illustrates a simple fact of life: You can't have total commitment because you don't always have total control. There are unknowns with everything in life, and there will always be times and occasions when you will not be able to maintain the commitment you have made on the job, to your boss, to clients, or even your family. How you handle these unknowns is the key to your influence on the results you want.

Priorities change daily, if not hourly. We are all dealing with human beings, who have families, health problems, and accidents. When something happens to them that they can't help, we adjust quickly. Not to be flexible enough to cope with situations like this can spell disaster for any project. Allowances must be made for the human equation, and a prior "plan" for such emergencies should always be in place.

People in the theatrical world are always ready for a breakdown. So when a show is produced, there are always understudies and "swings"—people on whom they can call to take a role when needed, people who have rehearsed and who are prepared.

Given this fact of life, we need to remember that all of those around us want to be committed but can't always do what they promise. This is not a reason to distrust them or their judgment; it is simply a factor we need to build into the plans we formulate because inevitably we will not achieve all our commitments and will need to make modifications and take alternate routes to achieve success. Even in A/E/C project management, we need understudies and "swings."

Commitment brings about several inherent benefits that help the team achieve the goals that have been established, from improved communication to getting the results you are looking for.

Commitment is a key ingredient to achieve success. Base your belief on the fact that the people you work with also want to be committed to the common goal. Think about what you can do to ensure success through your personal influence and what actions are necessary to achieve results. If you are the leader, it is up to you to make the plans, plan the backup, and inspire the team.

What can you do to ensure you are on the right track?

America has seen many changes. In the past, change came about slowly. Whatever the status quo may have been in those years, most people were not willing to accept change. The last 15 years have seen greater changes in America than in all of the years of its existence. Even those in small towns and villages, quiet corners of America, or in remote areas who have held on to their customary lifestyles have been affected by the changes that have come about in our country. But in business, change is inevitable, and rapid change is a fact of life. Those not willing to change may not be able to compete in the current business climate. What can you do to survive?

You must prepare yourself and your company to survive and thrive in the changing and evolving business environment. Finding solutions to the myriad issues and problems facing your segment of the business needs to be done at lower levels of the organizational chart than were previously ever considered. Downsizing has eliminated many organizational levels in many companies, and all individuals are now compelled to make their own decisions on the complex business dilemmas that develop on a recurring basis.

The entire team must now focus on common goals that your industry, business, and company must face daily. Unity of approach can help lessen the chance of ineffective decisions being made and minimize the potential for conflicts between individuals within or between departments. This effort will encourage more ingenuity from the team and will give them the opportunity to initiate ideas and solutions and enhance motivation. The net result for your company is a direct impact on your bottom line, improved productivity in the office and the field operations, and ultimately higher levels of quality for the finished product and a satisfied end user of your product or service.

Establishing a Climate of Success for Your Team

This section discusses what you can do as an employee, manager, or owner to improve your ability to get the results you want. There is no easy fix or solution. It takes time and concerted effort on your part to get others to take the actions you want them to take on your behalf. Everyone is distinctly different, therefore the methods will vary for each individual or department you are striving to influence. What you must keep in mind is the reality that you alone control the ability to make the changes necessary to effect the results you seek.

Mission statements

The concept of developing the right *mission statement* for your company is an important management tool. Without one, you are traveling an unknown road without a map. If you, as a leader or manager, don't know where you're going, how would you expect your staff to know? The statement should be short, provocative, and inspiring. From your local government to subcontractors, everyone struggles with the effort to define for themselves the perfect mission statement. In many ways, the presence of a mission statement is viewed as a panacea for all that ails most companies. The mission statement is simply your company's philosophy. It is what your company does and why it does it. You may already have a mission or a philosophy in your head. But if you write it down and share it with your employees and customers, they will help make it possible to reach your goals.

Your employees must know where the company is going in order for them to help drive it there. If they understand your mission, their decision-making becomes easier, more focused, and more organizationally cohesive. In addition, the makeup of your staff begins to take shape. Some individuals do not fit with some company missions. They may choose to adjust or to find a match somewhere else. You want people on your team who are willing to support your mission.

When your clients and prospective clients know your company's mission, they know exactly what to expect from you. They know what you do, what you stand for, and why they should or should not do business with you.

There are several great books on the market that will help you write a mission statement in a concise manner, focusing on issues such as your position in the marketplace, defining the business you are in, identifying your target market, and crystallizing your company philosophy.

After you have written your mission statement, ask yourself one question: Could any of my competitors use this statement? If they can, you're not finished with your task. Your mission statement must include your differences from your competitors, what makes your company stand out from the field.

Mission statements are not always the perfect solution to providing company direction. Most of the time they are never used once developed, or they have been created by upper management to be followed only by the troops in the trenches. Mission statements that are created by everyone in the entire organization and are inbred as a company philosophy have a greater chance of succeeding—and consequently, so will the company. The mission statement must be relevant to your core business, must be implemented, and must be a part of daily operations—a real working tool.

If you really want to galvanize the efforts of your team, you must go a step further by developing a *vision statement*. Vision statements are less specific than a mission statement. They are a statement of what you will become as a company if you repeatedly and successfully accomplish your mission. You create your vision by asking, "What will accomplishing our mission do for our company, our industry, and our community? What impact will we have?"

Think of the company you most admire of all those you currently deal with (supplier, client, competitor, etc.). Why does it stand out? It is likely that the employees have a common sense of purpose. The company's business dealings always have favorable results. The company and its employees always do a good job. It contributes time or money to the community. It is considered responsible, trustworthy, and reliable. Its people always comport themselves in a fair and ethical manner. The company's reputation is impeccable. The company can be counted on to do what it says it will do. Put that all together, and you have the makings of a very good vision statement. Tailor it to suit your own ideas and tastes, and get your employees to contribute to it. With this in hand, you will notice that the attitude of the entire team will improve.

Don't be afraid to beat a path for employees to follow. They generally thrive when they know exactly where they are going.

Chapter

4

Research Is the Foundation of Your Marketing Plan

An article in *Engineering News-Record* stated that pressure never lets up on A/E/C officers and their firms regarding the implementation of information technology in the new millennium by leveraging computers and communications effectively.

If you are still not sold on the importance of computer technology and research as it effects business and the general public, consider the online search by a private investigator on a person whom he had been hired to investigate, which gathered "a five- page computer printout from just her name. The investigator had found her Social Security number, date of birth, every address at which she had ever resided, the names and telephone numbers of past and present neighbors, even the number of bedrooms in a house she had inherited, her welfare history, and the work histories of her children's fathers." And he was just getting started.

Information technology has created an invaluable resource for us. As in the 20th century, when a national highway system was developed and soon linked all urban and rural areas, technological advances have done much the same thing in recent years. Old rules for and methods of finding information to plan, enhance, and perform our business lives are taking the form of an electronic "hot button" that can tap any question, answer any inquiry, or solve any problem we may encounter. The advent of a new highway system resulted in the reduction of our past reliance on railroads and shipping lines, just as the Internet has reduced our dependence on fax machines, telephones, and print media.

The building industry has experienced a radical shift in the paradigms we view as the norms for business. Those firms that have mastered this means of doing business will thrive and grow. We can't imagine that there are many entrepreneurs who haven't realized the wisdom of using tools their competitors use so successfully. But if there are some, competition will surely prove to be too stiff. The workplace has evolved into a combination of home, office, and road, creating a "connected and linked" lifestyle for those brave enough to venture out into it.

An amazing fact is that the typical individual of the 1800s was rarely exposed in his or her entire lifetime to what is published today in the average daily newspaper. We are experiencing information glut, with news and advertising coming at us from all directions.

When desktop computers first arrived on the scene, it was a shock to the average office worker. Change is frightening, and this was unprecedented change, not exactly welcome to most companies and to most employees. There were shockwaves throughout the country and around the world. During that period, when people were being interviewed for jobs, some protested. "Oh, no! I've never used a computer and I don't intend to." Some employees insisted that a desktop computer was the "work of the devil." But then, they used to say that about automobiles, and telephones! Nevertheless, the 1980s found companies adapting to this new technology, first reluctantly, then enthusiastically as they came to realize that this new tool could be beneficial, would produce more work in a shorter amount of time with fewer people, and with greater economy and profitability.

Companies have made the transition from using computers strictly for accounting estimation to using them for construction services, such as voice recognition for daily logs by superintendents. Leaving their comfortable and familiar bases to update and modify existing systems had to be extremely stressful for many firms. However, in the last few years, principals have realized that without the latest hardware and software, production, and communications technologies—and without workers trained in today's most sophisticated computer skills—it is impossible to be competitive in the marketplace.

Small firms traditionally have had a distinct advantage over larger firms in this area. They are able to upgrade and retrofit their existing technology easier and faster than larger firms are. Less overhead expense and politics gives small firms the agility to make quick changes to their in-house resources. This modification of technology will allow them to provide more quality and speed to the end product for their clients and will promote a new interconnectivity for their consultants, all the while easing the transition from in-house staff to a much more flexible situation with outsourcing to professions on a temporary basis. The net results for companies that can achieve this transformation will be that they become highly price competitive and much more productive and efficient with their overall operations. This can provide a considerable competitive advantage because it sets firms apart from their competition.

The explosion of electronic data is a natural extension of the rapid changes and advancements in the technological world. Barely a decade has passed since the microchip transformed the way we think about, analyze, and transact business. Now, business owners can connect remotely to all office workstations and branch offices.

Research began initially with the development of local networks to improve data sharing and office communications. Not too much time passed before management discovered the advantages of easy access to posted project schedules, job estimates, and projections using sophisticated software programs.

Many companies are maintaining dynamic and constantly changing schedules for immediate feedback of personnel and resources. Supplementing such devices are other in-house resources—daily logs and reports, timesheets, payroll, change orders, RFIs, submittals, and job photography—as well as outside resources, such as industry reports, company RFPs, and all sorts of data available from many web sites. The A/E/C world has much to gain from technology. Current technology allows the documentation and regular monitoring of activities in real-time mode for all levels of job implementation. Top executives of most companies are fully aware that the capital investment in equipment and training is worth the effort and money. The phenomenal growth of many A/E/C firms proves it. Managers consider it mandatory that their employees, both those at headquarters and branch offices and those in the field, are equipped with the latest and best of the gadgets that keep them in touch with the home office, making it possible for them to be contacted when needed, and be available when called upon to solve critical problems.

Today, most workers carry cell phones, personal digital assistants, and pagers. When these people are needed, they are expected to be available, no matter where they are—on the road, at home, or on vacation. Time is money. Information is money. The knowledge and technical skills that are inside a key worker's head are money. No longer is an employee on an "eight-hour shift." Many key workers are on call 24-7. Workers have computers at home, an e-mail connection with the office, files at home, and access to whatever new concept surfaces, such as voice recognition technology. Companies are prepared to do whatever it takes to bring a project in on time and under budget. Whatever they invest in technology to make that possible is considered a necessary investment.

Marketing Research: Building Your Foundation to Protect Your Assets

What a difference a few years can make. Only a few years ago most of us, as we pursued information about clients or a new territory, would go to our friendly neighborhood library, sit down at the card catalog, and search for topics relevant to the areas we needed. Subject, title, and author were the parameters, and the librarian would help with this series of quests. Usually the information was stored somewhere else, and we would have to return to review it later. We would sift through magazines or view the information on microfilm. The days of such contemplative research are over, and none too soon. Such techniques will no longer suit the world we now live in. The availability of the Internet to millions of people has shaken up the world of information vendors as they attempt to compete with free search sites such as AltaVista, Google, and Yahoo.

The ease of using search sites is impressive. Anywhere you go, computers are available for you to log in, and travel as far as you need to in order to find the information you need. And, of course, if you carry a laptop with you, it becomes easier yet. Your hand curled around the handle of your own portable computer means you're a fingertip away from an entire world of information.

Planning a research program for your company

Whatever your strategic plan, there are many excellent research methods available to you on the Internet. Staff development, competitor research, market expansion, personnel background checks, monitoring market share, keeping up with the latest trends and developments within your segment of the building industry—all of this and more can be organized by your company. However, before you go surfing, following random leads, save yourself some time and create a work outline such as the following.

Identify the information you are specifically looking for. Brainstorm with fellow staff, existing clients, prospective clients, and local trade associations. Prepare a list of potential sources from which to obtain the statistics and data you need. Gather the information and organize it by topic and subtopic. After you have gathered a significant amount of information, meet with your office staff again, review the information you have found, try to identify the areas that need additional support, and see if there are new areas to cover. Continue the search process to fill in the blanks. Meet again with your company team to assimilate the information, summarize it, and determine whether a conclusion can be drawn. Recognize that the information you have assembled will resonate differently with each individual in the group. Note that each may offer a different and valuable interpretation, and may offer you information on where you can find additional important details. Use this checklist:

1. Identify information.

2. Brainstorm with staff and others.

3. Prepare a list of resources.

4. Gather and sort the information.

5. Meet with staff again. Determine what's missing.

6. Continue the search.

7. Meet with the staff again, review information, and get input.

Start developing your strategic plan based upon the research you have gathered and the input of your colleagues. Research takes time and labor, but the results will be focused and based on fact, and they can provide the direction needed to make the serious decisions necessary for creating a strategic plan with the real potential to improve your bottom line.

Developing a plan is critical to the success of any research you decide to conduct. It will provide an organized roadmap to use to collect and analyze information, and timetables to follow to achieve the end product. The plan will help you make better marketing decisions.

The driving goal of all research is to help the company increase its revenue. A company that is about to undertake a marketing research project of any size is well advised to consider, during the initial planning sessions, its strengths, weaknesses, opportunities, and direct market threats, otherwise known as a SWOT analysis. Such an analysis provides a method for the team to systematically review the internal and external elements that have a direct influence over a company's success. **Figure 4.1** is a sample SWOT analysis.

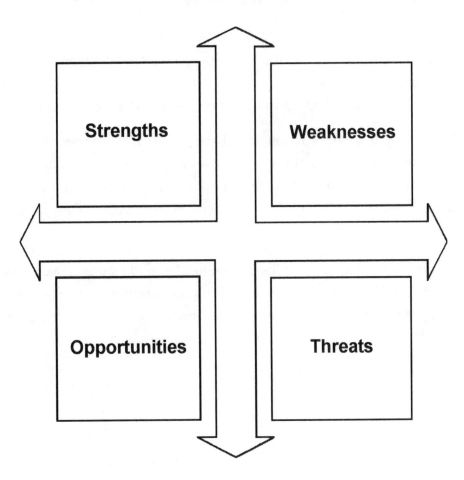

Figure 4.1. SWOT analysis.

Strengths

- ◆ Average experience of individuals in the firm is eight years
- ◆ Expertise in stadium structures
- ◆ Repeat business with 75 percent of client base
- ◆ Able to adjust to changing market conditions

Weaknesses

- No marketing plan has been developed
- Limited experience in a new major market segment
- Large number of new employees with no experience
- Low repeat business ratio

Opportunities

- No direct competitor in institutional market segment
- Successful completion of current work in a new market area
- Strong networking ability within regional associations

Threats

- Three new firms moving into the area with specific market experience
- Low unemployment rate
- New procurement methods to which the company has limited exposure

Once a SWOT analysis has been accomplished, the process will become simpler. However, as research takes inordinate amounts of time, don't start in the middle of your busy season. Plan ahead and begin the process when you have the time to devote your full attention to this important task. Technology has simplified many aspects of this process so that it can be done systematically and perhaps more easily than before.

Set priorities and proceed systematically. Try not to take on too much at once. Assign portions to your staff and support personnel. Establish your priorities. As you go about your regular daily assignments, meetings, preparation of estimates and proposals, and general problem solving, you may encounter pieces of the research puzzle to be added.

Using the Web for Information Gathering

Now that you have completed the planning process with your team, reviewing existing market conditions, company position, potential environmental forces, and the specific information you want to research, another enormous amount of information is available to you.

It's a rare company that doesn't have an Internet connection these days. However, if you still haven't committed to this form of communication, you should. There are hundreds, if not thousands, of Internet providers throughout the country. You can get a connection for a modest sum that will provide you with the ability to search the Internet, design your own personal web site, and have an e-mail address.

Another alternative is to develop a personal Internet address with your Internet provider. For less than $50 per year you can have your own company registered; you can reserve your domain name now through Network Solutions (www.networksolutions.com). This website also allows you to check the entire Internet to see if your name is available by using its "WHOIS" link. What is even more amazing is that you can be up and running in less than 24 hours. Needless to say, this is for a very basic site. Sites can easily run from thousands of dollars for companies wanting to make a grand statement to much more for a one-of-a-kind, complex, graphically intense site.

Internet search tools

There are many browsers available, and selecting one is a personal matter. The two leading browsers are Microsoft Internet Explorer and Netscape Navigator. Both can be downloaded from the Internet at no cost for a trial period.

A browser feature that might interest you is called "off-line browsing." It allows individuals to download to their desktop computer a web site of their choosing and access it at their own pace. This can speed the process of access and is an easier way to access that web site in the future. Changes that have occurred to the web site since it was downloaded to the desktop will be automatically updated when you access it online again in the future.

For marketing research of information on the web, each search engine has its own strengths and unique characteristics. You'll need to experiment with each and see which one fits your specific needs during that particular search. Another simple method of saving the sites you discover during your research is to mark them. Right-click on them with the mouse. This will allow you to save them as your favorite sites.

Yahoo! (www.yahoo.com) is the largest and most well known of the directories on the World Wide Web; it was the original pioneer search index. You can search for anything using this tool, and it will provide you with an index of potential sites.

Search engines differ from directories in that they search the web pages looking for words that match the words used in your marketing research. This is slowly taming the Internet beast by allowing you to find all references to the topics you search for; the drawback is that you can uncover thousands of sites that match your search specifics. You need to find methods to narrow your search so that you are not flooded with sites that have no or limited importance. Utilizing a *Boolean search* methodology can direct and focus your research efforts. Keywords such as AND, OR, and NEAR can enhance your search (see **Figure 4.2**).

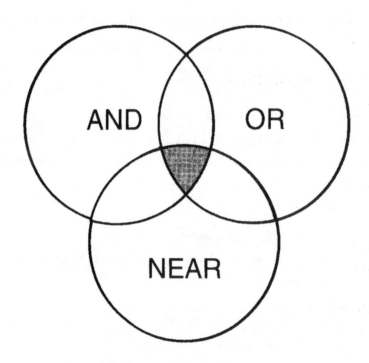

Figure 4.2. Boolean search.

A few examples of Boolean search strings follow:

♦ Economic Development AND Cleveland: ensures that both terms are present in documents searched for

♦ Associated General Contractors OR AGC: ensures that at least one of these two terms is present

♦ City Hall NEAR Boston: ensures that these two terms are within 10 words of each other

Listed below are some of the industry search engines that have a reputation for getting you positive results. Each has a distinct advantage in the research process.

♦ **4specs.com**—search engine for specified construction products; provides access to more than 10,000 manufacturer's web sites (www.4specs.com)

♦ **AEC Info**—fast and easy access to more than 300,000 pages of building material information including specifications and CAD details (www.aecinfo.com)

♦ **AltaVista**—large, well-known search engine with minimal advertising (www.altavista.com)

♦ **Amazing Environmental Organization WebDirectory**—earth's biggest environment search engine (www.webdirectory.com)

♦ **BigFoot**—White Pages search engine (www.bigfoot.com)

♦ **BuildFind**—comprehensive directories containing building-industry organizations and resources (www.buildfind.com)

♦ **BuildingOnline**—compiles thousands of web pages in categories such as architects, associations, contractors, and wholesalers (www.buildingonline.com)

♦ **Construction Equipment**—directories of equipment dealers, manufacturers, specifications, and trade names (www.constructionequipment.com)

♦ **Contractors Hot Line**—nationwide database of construction equipment for sale. Includes an equipment locator and price guide, auction results, and state department of transportation bids and lettings (www.contractorshotline.com)

♦ **eLibrary**—subscription-based research too offering comprehensive access to an archive of more than 17 million documents (www.elibrary.com)

♦ **Excite**—like Yahoo!, allows you to search by concept or single word a vast archive of material (www.excite.com)

♦ **Go.com**—comprehensive web site similar to Excite and Yahoo! (www.go.com)

♦ **Google**—large, well-known search engine that searches more than three billion web pages (www.google.com)

♦ **HotBot**—this site can make the Internet universe more manageable (www.hotbot.com)

♦ **Internet @ddress Finder**—a good place to start if you're looking for Internet addresses, area or zip codes, or similar information (www.iaf.net)

♦ **Lycos**—highly rated search engine, developed by Carnegie Mellon University, that permits you to zero in on your competitor's web sites to find out how they position themselves (www.lycos.com)

♦ **SHAREWARE.com**—search engine for shareware programs and free software (www.shareware.com)

♦ **SuperPages**—expansive directory including Yellow and White Pages for U.S. businesses (www.superpages.com)

Some of the sites mentioned above are general and broad ranging. Some are related to the building and construction industry. If your discipline is, for instance, engineering, landscape architecture, interior design, or one of the many disciplines related to architecture, engineering, and construction, there are similar listings in each of the disciplines. Simply enter the category in which you are interested, but narrow the search as much as you can or you will come up with thousands of listings, too many for the average person to handle.

Most search engines are divided into two general types: indexed or category-based. Indexed search engines, such as AltaVista and Excite, use automated web crawlers to index the words on web pages. You enter key words in a box on the search page, and the engine returns links to pages that contain those words. Many engines support full-text searching of the sites included in their databases. Others go even further by indexing certain fields as well (such as title, author, and abstract) similar to a traditional library.

A category-based search engine such as Yahoo! has a staff of reviewers who organize web sites into a hierarchical structure. Instead of searching for specific words on a web page, these engines search for words in a category name or site summary. The search results begin with general categories that branch into more detailed subcategories. Category-based searches are useful for collecting general information on a topic quickly. To find information about topics that aren't so easily categorized, you would do better to use an indexed search site.

The following listings are a good starting point if you need additional information on search engines, plus additional methods to refine your search. Each of these sites has its own advantages and benefits for your research activities.

♦ **Internet Searching Strategies**—site developed by Rice University to help students utilize the Internet; easy to navigate, it provides a step-by-step approach to maximizing research activities (www.rice.edu/Fondren/Netguides/strategies.html)

♦ **Metacrawler**—this site doesn't depend on one search engine but many, and thus has the potential of allowing you to find more information pertaining to your particular subject; it also strives to rank the information it provides (www.metacrawler.com)

♦ **ProFusion**—a search engine for Internet search engines developed at Kansas University, the program helps narrow the search to specific terms within a title of a web site and to terms within a specific page without representation (www.profusion.com)

♦ **Search Engine Watch**—explains in detail how search engines index web sites and provides search engine descriptions, reviews, and tutorials; sign up for a free newsletter to keep up with new search engines (www.searchenginewatch.com)

Associations

Associations are often overlooked as a source of information. Industry associations can furnish you with a variety of data to facilitate comprehensive market research. Most associations can provide calendars, back issues of publications, contacts for staff members, and information on current code and regulatory issues. Many have a help line that offers the opportunity to ask questions regarding particular issues.

♦ **American Council of Engineering Companies** (www.acec.org)
♦ **American Institute of Architects** (www.aia.org)
♦ **American Institute of Steel Construction** (www.aisc.org)
♦ **American Marketing Association** (www.ama.org)
♦ **American Society of Civil Engineers** (www.asce.org)
♦ **American Society of Concrete Contractors** (www.ascconline.org)
♦ **American Society of Mechanical Engineers** (www.asme.org)
♦ **American Wood Council** (www.awc.org)
♦ **Associated Builders and Contractors** (www.abc.org)
♦ **Associated General Contractors of America** (www.agc.org)

- ♦ **ASTM International (formerly American Society for Testing & Materials)** (www.astm.org)
  - ♦ **Construction Specifications Institute** (www.csinet.org)
  - ♦ **Greater San Antonio Builders Association** (www.sabuilders.com)
  - ♦ **Institute of Electrical and Electronics Engineers, Inc.** (www.ieee.org)
  - ♦ **National Association of Home Builders** (www.nahb.com)
  - ♦ **National Institute of Building Sciences** (www.nibs.org)
  - ♦ **National Society of Professional Engineers** (www.nspe.org)
  - ♦ **Service Corps of Retired Executives** (www.score.org)
  - ♦ **Society for Marketing Professional Services** (www.smps.org)
  - ♦ **Urban Land Institute** (www.uli.org)
  - ♦ **Washington Building Congress** (www.wbcnet.org)

Government databases

Government databases can provide the statistics you may need on a new market territory, market size, or potential revenue sources.

- ♦ **FedBizOpps**—the single government point-of-entry for federal government procurement opportunities over $25,000 (www.fedbizopps.gov)

- ♦ **Federal Trade Commission**—offers good links to other business-oriented sites (www.ftc.gov)

- ♦ **Fedmarket.com**—online community for government buyers and vendors (www.fedmarket.com)

- ♦ **FedWorld.gov**—managed by the National Technical Information Service, this site is a gateway to government information (www.fedworld.gov)

- ♦ **House of Representatives** (www.house.gov)

- ♦ **Library of Congress**—online information on books about the building industry (www.loc.gov)

- ♦ **Occupational Safety and Health Administration** (www.osha.gov)

- ♦ **Securities and Exchange Commission**—includes access to the Edgar database, which contains the full text of reports that public companies are required to file with the SEC, including quarterly financial statements (www.sec.gov)

◆ **Small Business Administration** (www.sba.gov)

◆ **THOMAS**—official source of U.S. legislative information on the Internet (http://thomas.loc.gov)

◆ **U.S. Business Advisor**—gateway to government resources for business. (www.business.gov)

◆ **U.S. Census Bureau**—supplies a large volume of statistical data regarding locations within the United States (www.census.gov)

◆ **ZIP Code Lookup**—ZIP+4 information, compliments of the U.S. Postal Service (www.usps.gov/ncsc/lookups/lookup_zip+4.html)

Resource sites

Listed below are several industry web sites that can provide background research material for your next marketing plan or budget.

◆ **Advertising Age**—Information on advertising and marketing, plus the latest in marketing news (www.adage.com)

◆ **American Demographics**—learn where to focus your marketing efforts (www.americandemographics.com)

◆ **Bizjournals**—source for a number of local papers that focus on business news and development; including information on markets you may be considering moving into (www.bizjournals.com)

◆ **BusinessWire**—information, primarily in the form of press releases, about American companies both large and small (www.businesswire.com)

◆ **Dun & Bradstreet**—with a database of millions of U.S. businesses, this site offers tips on a variety of business-related topics and information on many public corporations, including background reports complete with sales figures, employee information, markets, and special promotional events (www.dunbradstreet.com)

◆ **Hoover's Online** —a limitless site that provides information about thousands of companies (www.hoovers.com)

- **IndustryLink**—excellent compilation of links to industry web sites (www.industrylink.com)

- **McGraw-Hill Construction**—this site includes links to a wealth of construction information, including the company's Dodge and Sweets products, and an online bookstore with more than 2,000 titles of books and software for the construction industry (www.construction.com)

- **Minority Business & Professional Directory**—thorough directory of businesses owned by minorities and women (www.mbpd.com)

- **Online Resources for the Construction Industry**—sign up for the free e-mail newsletter (www.copywriter.com/constr.htm)

- **PR Newswire**—Excellent source of press releases for thousands of companies (www.prnewswire.com)

- **PSMJ Resources, Inc.**—lists free offerings as well as marketing and consulting publications and seminars that are available for a fee (www.psmj.com)

- **Reed Construction Data**—billed as "construction information at its best," this site includes numerous products, including Clark Reports, Daily Commercial News, First Source, and the RSMeans product line (www.reedconstructiondata.com)

- **ThomasRegister**—online resource listing U.S. manufacturers, including information on millions of individual products, services, and companies (www.thomasregister.com)

Publications

The following publications can be read on line.

- **Architectural Record** (www.archrecord.com)

- **BusinessWeek** (www.businessweek.com)

- **Design Intelligence** (www.di.net)

- **Engineering News-Record** (www.enr.com)

- **Metropolis** (www.metropolismag.com)

Company web sites

Listed below are some of the best company web sites in the A/E/C industry. These illustrate ideas you may want to incorporate into your own web pages.

- **Andersen Windows** (www.andersenwindows.com)
- **Bentley Systems** (www.bentley.com)
- **Ellerbe Becket** (www.ellerbebecket.com)
- **3D International** (www.3di.com)
- **HNTB Corp.** (www.hntb.com)
- **Marvin Windows** (www.marvin.com)
- **National Gypsum Company** (www.national-gypsum.com)
- **Steelcase** (www.steelcase.com)

Newsgroups

Newsgroups function on the Internet as a public forum. Groups of people post and read messages on a particular topic of interest and then make comments if they have something of interest to add. They can be a good source of information. The information is shared among the group for support and assistance. Newsgroups allow you to get the inside track on your competition by monitoring rumors, and by providing good business intelligence practices.

Usenet, now part of the search engine company Google, is the most well-known newsgroup (www.groups.google.com). Some basic Usenet hierarchies marketed with the suffix of the group's name and end with:

- alt (alternative topics)
- biz (business)
- comp (hardware, software, and consumer info)
- misc (miscellaneous topics)
- news (information about Usenet News)
- rec (recreation)
- sci (science)
- soc (social issues)
- talk (current issues and debates)

These groups concentrate on segments of the market or types of companies, and also focus on trends. You should consider trying one. Then you might want to join by offering help and asking your own questions. A good program to test is Forte's Agent, which provides you with access to hundreds of messages each day. You can use one of the search engines to sort the information (www.forteinc.com).

Managing Data Using Lists

An easy and efficient method of doing a marketing research project that will pay dividends immediately is the use of effective lists of all pertinent aspects of your marketing plan. Good lists can simplify the entire marketing and service components of your business by giving you the ability to put the information you have cultivated, organized, and maintained into a format that can be easily managed and read by your office team. It is amazing how often marketers keep information in a small phone book in which numbers are scribbled and barely legible. The uses and benefits of well arranged and accessible lists to complement your marketing strategy are endless.

During your initial planning meeting, a discussion should be held on what types of lists would help the organization achieve its targeted goals and who will develop, select, and maintain these lists once they are created. It cannot be stressed often enough how important lists such as the following can be to your firm and to you:

1. *Clients/customers.* This is the first list that comes to mind. Look around your office. Can you lay your hands on a copy of your client list, with the names of the key participants, the history of the relationship, current projects under consideration or in construction, or a comparison of initial project estimates versus final executed results? This is the first place to start.

2. *Competitors.* This is another critical list to develop and maintain in order to monitor your competitors on a day-to-day basis. Who are their key employees, what are their strengths and weaknesses, what is their current client base and project backlog?

3. *Prospects.* Rank these lists by probability, size, complexity, margin potential, worker requirements, location, and interrelated companies or projects.

4. *Subcontractors and vendors.* Rate each by level of service, products, key individuals, past experiences, and areas of expertise.

5. *Print and electronic media.* These lists can facilitate an easy, quick distribution of press releases, newsworthy activities, and invitations to current company events.

6. *Supplemental references.* This could include accountants, lawyers, associations, governmental regulators (i.e., OSHA), local politicians, and planning agencies.

There are endless resources for your search and activities in developing a list. Once started, you can enlist the support and assistance of everyone in the office, especially if they are all linked by a server or intranet. Maintenance and diligent pruning to avoid duplication will be necessary, but the result will be an immensely powerful tool everyone in the office can utilize, and it will focus attention on key clients, competitors, and prospects so that the entire team is working toward a common direction for the company. Well-developed lists can be a valuable asset for any professional services firm as well as one of the foundations of a successful marketing program.

Low-Cost Surveys and Audits

Low-cost surveys and audits are another method of market research. There are any number of consultants who specialize in the development of marketing consulting and the use of surveys to obtain the information clients need for their strategic marketing plans. Here are some survey methods.

1. *Personal interviewing.* One-on-one or with focus groups. (Some of our colleagues use this method extensively in meeting with potential and current clients and competitors to obtain answers to marketing questions.) The company gathers the data and tabulates them by utilizing key quotations from interviews and looking for patterns, trends, and new opportunities.

2. *Telephone surveys.* This can be an effective method to obtain information quickly on a topic or subject of interest.

3. *Mailed questionnaires.* These generally have the lowest level of response by the selected groups. Following up with a phone call to request a response may enhance results. A method that usually gets better-than-average results is to make a one-page survey that can be faxed back to the sender. This seems to simplify the process and eliminates the middle step of adding an envelope and stamp.

The American Council for Construction Education utilized a survey on the *Engineering News-Record* web site for eliciting information on a Future Education Forum. All construction-related associations were notified and their members, at their own convenience, answered the questions listed. The answers were downloaded to the Civil Engineering Research Foundation for correlation and analysis. This resulted in minimal effort, maximum exposure, and a broad coverage of the market.

It's necessary to use not only computers to find and sort information, but also skilled personnel who know what they are looking for and can analyze the results. A poorly defined problem or an inadequate sequence of steps to uncover the information will not bring the right answers. The initial planning stage is critical to the final resolution. We have all heard the saying "garbage in, garbage out." A concerted effort to focus the research at the beginning will greatly enhance the end product.

A significant trend for construction companies is to enhance the staff's research productivity. More and more companies are attempting to minimize the number of personnel in their offices by downsizing, so they require more participation in decision-making from the remaining staff. Asking for input from staff members at the outset of the research process and getting opinions from staff as the process proceeds will be beneficial to the result. People resent being told what to do with the attitude "Ask no questions. You don't need to know." Every person on your staff has good ideas, access to good information, and through their personal contacts, information about the market that you might like to know. So utilize your staff intelligently. They could be your greatest asset.

Database Management for Intelligent Marketing Research Decisions

After the recession of the 1990s, we all learned quickly that to stay in business we had to cut costs and sell more services and products. A major trend has evolved called relationship marketing; it allows companies to base their direct-marketing efforts on extensive marketing databases. Companies that are doing well today collect detailed information about individual customers. Database marketing is the preferred method in the A/E/C community in order to understand clients' needs and to target only the most likely prospects.

Companies today can develop in-house, through an aggressive database marketing methodology, the information needed to reduce expenses while increasing revenue. It is not inexpensive or easy to develop. Developing and maintaining the database and ensuring that the information is entered regularly and correctly is essential. Information is located all over the company and all over the world. But databases can place your firm ahead of the curve and always in the path of additional orders.

Intelligence gathering and research are critical elements in effective marketing. All firms have in place some form of marketing information system that connects the external environment with their executives. It is even more important to provide that link at all levels of the organization. The research must have input from everyone and must be shared by everyone. Leave anyone out of the information loop, and you've rendered that person ineffective. Full participation is key.

A good marketing information system should be divided into four parts:

1. An *internal reports system* provides current data on accounts receivable and payable, sales, costs, executions, margins, safety results, and cash flow. Construction and design firms have in place elaborate job-cost accounting systems that, due to the advanced development of this segment of the office environment, are being enhanced and slowly distributed to all members of the team. Buy-in and performance-based bonus structures have allowed this information segment to reach a new maturity.

2. A *research gathering marketing intelligence system* is one that supplies executives with everyday information about what is going on in the external marketing environment. This can range from reading the newspaper to accessing a website for a projection of current projects with a breakdown on what they are, who owns them, who is building them, and where they are located. A well-trained marketing and sales team can obtain data from one of the online resources, hire a marketing consultant, or utilize its staff for special intelligence-gathering activities. This can greatly improve the information that company executives receive.

3. A *marketing research system* involves collecting information that has been targeted for research because of a perceived threat to or opportunity within the company. This process takes five steps: defining the problem and thoroughly narrowing the research objectives, developing a marketing research plan, gathering information in both internal and external markets, analyzing the material and data gathered, and presenting the findings and results to management and the entire staff.

4. An *analytical marketing system* usually is conducted by outside consultants with a staff of statisticians who run the data through advanced statistical procedures and models based on similar studies and researches for comparison, analysis, and dissection.

Chapter

5

Creating Your Marketing Plan

It used to be the case that there was little said, written, or published about marketing. The A/E/C industry had no thoughts of marketing as a necessary function. The perception of marketing in the early 1970's for the building industry was promotion driven. It was an ad hoc project-oriented effort. We did some modest advertising, a few brochures, and reluctantly made some cold calls. Long-term planning was not thought of. What we were doing was considered the leading-edge marketing effort for the industry, and it satisfied most business owners. Sales were the consuming activity. Estimating, pricing, bidding, estimating, pricing, bidding, estimating, pricing, bidding—that was the common perception of what you needed to do to get business.

A lawyer opened an office, hung up his shingle, and waited for business. He'd have his name listed in the local telephone book. It was considered unprofessional, outrageous, or even unethical to "market." The concept that marketing could apply to "professional" occupations was revolutionary, but suddenly there was a radical shift in the business environment as professionals such as attorneys, doctors, accountants, architects, engineers, and contractors realized that they needed visibility or their hope for future income would diminish, and ultimately the years of education, financial investment in a career, and hopes for success would be completely eradicated unless they took some active part in their own promotion. Until this time, these occupations were considered *above* this seemingly unprofessional approach for getting new business.

Suddenly, television and radio commercials were rife with professional advertising. Suddenly, print ads were visible everywhere. There were shockwaves. *What were these lawyers and doctors thinking of? Was this ethical, moral, in "good taste"?* The business environment had been simmering with dissatisfaction, and the reaction was not only revolutionary, but also sudden. Professionals were out there. It was no longer considered "poor taste" to announce in the media that you had a service to offer, that you were a skilled professional, you were open for business, and you would continue to tell the world that you are here to serve.

The gurus of the business world jumped in and validated the new professional position. The concept was legitimized by Peter Drucker, the famous management expert and author of many books (*The Essential Drucker; The Effective Executive*), when he wrote that the sole purpose of business is to create a customer, and that business has only two basic functions: marketing and *innovation*. No one's name meant more in the business world of the 1980s than Drucker's. So, when he supported the marketing concept, the public listened. The concept took root and blossomed in the '80s and '90s because by that time there were dozens of management books expounding upon the power and vital necessity of marketing for the financial health of an organization. Books such as *In Search of Excellence, A Passion for Excellence*, and *Megatrends* each stressed the concept of "what business are you really in?"

It was also in 1981 that Jack Miller—a civil engineer from Houston, TX, who founded the Jack Miller Network, has been organizing successful seminars for years, and won the Silver Hard Hat Award from the Construction Writers Association—wrote about the importance of the marketing plan: "A company without a plan is like a ship without a rudder. It moves aimlessly in the marketplace reacting to pipe dreams instead of real opportunities." His belief was that once this plan was in place, you could then start the mystical marketing process of making things happen. These thoughts were well circulated among companies across the country, and were influenced by the development of many company planning guides.

Another industry leader in the 1980s was Hank Parkinson of Parkinson and Associates in Austin, TX, who wrote an article for CSI about successful company executives who understood the importance of marketing. Parkinson found that most executives were involved with marketing 50 to 70 percent of their business lives, and rewarded those around them who did the same.

Our own experience follows this concept. Many times, technically savvy companies have lost out to the firm that had superior marketing skills, one in which its executives know what the market and its clients want. While they are able to deliver services on time and within budget, their strength is in customer relationships. This gives them an edge on the next project. Successful companies are not focused on being a "bid machine," but strive to focus their time and attention on a few quality client companies and doggedly pursue them with high-quality service.

Has it ever occurred to you, when a particular product clogs the airwaves and becomes the leader in its field, that possibly it's no better or worse than a similar product on the grocery shelf, but has reached its superior position because of superior marketing? Perhaps that is true of all business. Is Budweiser a better beer or are its executives better marketers? Aren't Pepsi and Coca-Cola exactly alike, or is it that the market leader is not necessarily the one that tastes "best," but the one that hits the airwaves the most often? If this is true of products, it's also true of services. Have you had great experiences with national purveyors of oil changes, haircuts, and insurance policies, or have you been brainwashed to believe that one is better because it is louder and more visible?

A Definition of Marketing: Perspectives

According to Gerre Jones, a well-known speaker and the author of *How to Market Professional Design Services* and other books, "Marketing defines, outlines, and sets the stage for sales. Marketing is to create or increase demand, to which sales, and profits, are the hoped-for results."

Theodore Levitt—former editor of *Harvard Business Review* and author of *The Marketing Imagination* and others—stresses that selling lets clients know what you have, whereas marketing strives to develop what the client wants at a price he or she will pay.

Ben Gerwick—civil and environmental engineer and author of *Construction of Offshore Structures* and other books—stated this premise in another way when he noted that marketing is an essential element in the survival and growth of design and construction organizations. He defines marketing as developing strong relationships that enable your company to sell its services in the most favorable places and with the best terms and time frames·

The American Marketing Association's Committee on Definitions says that marketing is "the performance of business activities that direct the flow of goods and services from producer to consumer or user."

Figure 5.1. Marketing mix.

Finally, Herman Holtz (author of numerous books on business and consulting) said, "Anyone can sell cold drinks to thirsty people. Marketing is the art of finding or inventing ways to make people thirsty."

These definitions create the idea that marketing is a direct step to customer satisfaction and provides customers with the goods, products, or services they want. The result is a handsome profit. How many times have you been in a meeting when the discussion turns to pushing a product or service that your company wants to sell but not necessarily what the market wants to buy? This is a common, universal dilemma. Marketing today has the mix shown in **Figure 5.1**.

If marketing is based on two basic beliefs—(1) that your company policies, operations, and planning should be oriented toward the customer; and (2) that profitable sales volume should be the ultimate end result of the marketing plan—marketing is finding methods to satisfy those client expectations and receiving a reasonable profit. The definition of marketing has evolved today into a total company philosophy that integrates and coordinates all marketing activities within all company operations for the fundamental purpose of maximizing the bottom line for the corporation. This is not an option; it is a mandate for any company whose owners want to be successful. Many company presidents believe that marketing is a simple process in which you hire a marketing director and watch contracts and money roll in. It rarely works that way.

Marketing is a much more extensive framework of resources and tools. Most new marketing directors take a year to get anything established. It takes at least that long for the marketing process they have developed to gain a foothold. Also, the new marketing manager needs many more tools and resources than a simple company credit card to be truly effective. The company as a whole must be committed to the marketing concept. Everyone in the organization must be a part of this marketing process and support it. Regular meetings to discuss the goals they want to achieve and to sum up results of its effort need to be scheduled. Additional marketing support material should be developed as an integral part of the marketing process. Direct mail pieces, the traditional company brochure, special marketing events, public relations activities, and industry involvement are all a part of the process.

Marketing people entering a new job in an engineering, architectural, construction, landscaping, or any professional firm face real challenges, even hazards. You're new, maybe new to the field, but certainly new to this firm, and you don't know the territory or the clients. So you go out to call on a few. You may have some handicaps, such as being young, or female, or blonde, or perhaps a minority. Let's face it. We do not live in a perfect world, and people have some extraordinary prejudices. So you walk in to an executive's office and find a gentleman who has perhaps come up in rough, tough times. Here you are trying to tell him that XYZ firm is capable of handling a multimillion-dollar project; and he looks at you as if you're crazy. "I don't want to talk to you, kid. Where's your boss?" And there's the crux of the situation. This person is *not* going to hand over that multimillion-dollar project to the new kid on the block unless the team behind the effort is visible and accessible, unless he knows who they are, what they do, what they've done before, and whether they can address his problems. So, if you want to get his business, you need the entire firm behind you. And that's the key.

This process—a plan, a team, complete backup, marketing materials—if implemented properly, can increase market share by 30 to 50 percent. But, before you jump right into marketing, you *must* plan. This is one step that almost everyone feels is inessential, but ignoring this process can result in chaos, confusion, and a dead end. It is not just important, but essential to plan. The plan must lay out what you need to do, when you need to do it, and how the top executives and the entire staff will back up that person whom they're sending into battle. The rewards and benefits of this step are numerous and extremely beneficial.

Achieving What You Want through Mission Statements

The first step in this process is the establishment of a mission statement. Just what do you want to accomplish? And where do you begin?

Scott Butcher, author and consultant with Butcher Consulting Group, York, PA, described the mission statement clearly when he said, "The mission statement is your destination. The marketing plan, in conjunction with the strategic plan, is your road map to get there."

This is echoed by Richard Sides, construction specialist and consultant with Strategies That Work, Grapevine, TX, who believes the corporate mission statement can be the most important segment of your marketing plan because it clarifies your company's primary priority—to attract and keep customers.

Important? You bet. This is the guiding light that directs your efforts. It also illustrates that everyone in the organization, not just the marketing team, is part of the solution. This helps to impress on everyone that a team approach to marketing and attention to satisfying the customer must be on everyone's mind.

Marketing Mix

The concept of the *marketing mix* has become the base from which marketing is developed within any company. The mix of activities that mesh the customer's wants and needs, integrated with other external environmental factors, will create a successful marketing program. It is this diagnosis that determines where your business is positioned compared to the rest of the industry. The careful evaluation of where your company is placed from the standpoint of the competition and in the perspective of your clients and potential clients is critical. Step back and take the time to examine this factor. It is important not to ignore this element of your plan and blind yourself to the perceptions that exist about you and your position in the industry. Remember, it doesn't matter what you think about your company; it is important to know how your company appears to your clients!

As you build your program and examine your marketing mix, keep this priority uppermost in your mind. Your chance for success will become much higher with this approach. It is simple, straightforward, and by far the most logical sequence for your marketing and sales effort. An existing service to an existing client who is satisfied and happy with your past relationship will always provide the greatest financial reward.

Situation Analysis

A situation analysis is one of the first steps you must take before beginning to assemble your marketing plan. The situation analysis is no more than looking at the current competitive environment, getting a clear view of where the company can grow, and learning what services, perceptions, resources, and clients your competition utilizes. You should compare this analysis to your own functions to see where the differences are. Review your position by comparison with the competition. Are you a market leader, a challenger, a follower, or a niche player? The analysis should include a discussion of prices, differentiation, barriers that exist to entry to your desired segment of the business, and the unique advantages you may have. What trends have come and gone? What segments of the market are thriving and why is that so? Which segments are doing poorly?

Analysis can be as complex and extensive as you may need, but generally the more compact and precise, the better it will be for the understanding of what has transpired during the past year.

You may at some point have hired a consultant to do a situational analysis for you and may have received a hefty report that landed somewhere on a shelf, without having been examined or read by anyone. Or you or others may have glanced at it briefly, and plunk! Right on a dusty shelf it went. If that is so, this is the time to take it out and read it. No matter how old it may be, summarize it in a few paragraphs and see to it that the entire team reads that summary. What have you learned? Does any of this material apply to the current situation? Have there been radical changes in the structure of your organization, and in its outlook? If you find anything of value in the old analysis, could it be a launching pad for a new one? Or could it serve as an outline? It's always wise to make use of existing information.

Whether or not you do have an existing analysis, you know that you need new information. Now it is time for a group analysis of where you are and where you're going. A thorough discussion of all segments of your business should be conducted with your office staff, clients, industry groups, and associations. The results of these discussions, along with a review and summary of the data uncovered in your initial research efforts, will paint a clear picture of what has transpired in the past year. An in-depth analysis of the strengths and weaknesses of the company is paramount. Regular up-to-date information on each competitor should be maintained in your company database. This should include photographs of your competitors' work and what your competitors' clients are saying about them. One of the greatest errors a firm can make, according to C. F. Culler Associates of Atlanta, is "overlooking the importance of this type of analysis, using general descriptions, and omitting market research that supports demand."

Here are some questions and issues to be addressed:

- What type of business are we in now, and where do we want to be in five to ten years?
- What is our current sales volume?
- What are our current profit goals, and are we making them consistently?
- What are our company's strengths?
- What are our company's weaknesses?
- What would we like to add to our scope of services and/or products?
- What type of potential clients are we looking for?
- What is our preferred way of doing business?
- What are our company goals now, and how have we reached them in the past?
- What assets and resources do we have with regard to people, equipment, and technical capabilities?
- What trends do we foresee within our internal and external market?
- Are we willing to expand geographically?

These questions can be organized in the form of a SWOT analysis that the entire organization can build around. This analysis systematically reviews all major internal and external environmental conditions that may affect your organization. Ideally, this inventory of your market should be conducted off-site in a retreat setting, where the entire staff can brainstorm and offer its own ideas and beliefs. The team should also update this inventory at least annually.

One company that has been very successful with situational analysis is the Disney Company. Author, biographer, and investment adviser Richard J. Maturi writes that Disney gathers a team together and uses "storyboarding to develop the history through the use of movable cards to organize and reorganize new and old ideas that flow from brainstorming sessions." This is a simple method of enabling an entire organization to participate in the marketing analysis, but still ensuring that the analysis is relevant to each segment of the company.

Market segmentation will follow the development of a company SWOT analysis. This is a placement of customers within the grids based on the strengths defined. It enables marketers to focus their time and plans on a targeted market group. This segmentation should illustrate a diverse group of client types that can be further analyzed based on profitability. An example of how this information may be laid out is shown in **Table 5.1.**

Client Type	Less than $1 million	$1-5 million	$5-10 million	Larger than $10 million
Institutional				
Commercial				
Design-build				
Lump sum				
Negotiated				
Interior				
Full construction				
Joint ventures				

Table 5.1. Market segmentation grid.

This table can be expanded to include the total market share and what your percentage of each is and where you believe it could be. The ultimate purpose of this process is to find homogeneous groupings of potential prospects whose requirements are essentially the same so that you can focus your marketing approach.

A review of the marketing life cycle is also an important step when making any decision at this stage of the planning process. Products and services are thought of as having a life that begins with their introduction, continues through the growth and maturity stages, and ends in decline. The potential life cycle of any product or service is important to keep in mind as your analysis takes form. Initially there is minimal competition when a new product or service is introduced, and the volume and profits of the introduction shows a curve that starts an upward incline. As the service or product goes into the growth phase, the curve moves upward. As the service or product reaches the mature state, inevitably there is a gradual and then a more severe decline. This is normal for any product. Needless to say, as you analyze your position with a situational analysis, you want to attempt to position yourself as close to the introduction of any new service or product's life cycle as possible. This ensures a moderate guarantee of a significant volume of business opportunities, and the opportunity to maximize your profit potential.

When you view the marketing strategies of commercial companies that sell products, you can see what they do with their life cycles. Observe the fast food industry, for instance. A new hamburger is introduced. It is marketed heavily. It reaches a peak as long as it stands alone. As soon as the competition gets in, the first hamburger reaches a plateau and begins to decline. Management introduces a new wrinkle, or a new product, or several new products in succession; or a new way of presenting the same old hamburger. View any product or service company in the world and you will see the same life cycle. To reach that high peak is an achievement. To keep it takes ingenuity, creativity, and imagination.

Product, Price, Promotion, and Place—The Four Ps

Marketing can be broken into four distinct and critical segments. It is important to achieve the proper balance among these for maximum results.

1. *Product.* The product or service that a company has designed to satisfy a client's needs. A conscious strategy must be in place to keep introducing new services so as to prolong the life of maturing products or services.

2. *Price.* The dollar value that has been finally exchanged for the product.

3. *Promotion.* The methods the company has utilized to inform potential buyers about the service or product. Make sure you convey a consistent message to your client at every point of contact.

4. *Place.* How a company delivers (distributes) the service or product to the consumer or client.

Strategies + Action Plans = Marketing Plan

The marketing plan is your road map to success in charting a five-year plan of action for your organization. Without one, you can get off course and waste considerable time, money, and resources. Most companies can't afford to do this in today's business arena. According to Frank Stasiowski, founder of PSMJ/Resources in Newton, MA, and lecturer, author/publisher of a number of business books, there are five elements necessary for a successful marketing strategy: (1) marketplace analysis; (2) researching the client; (3) understanding how your firm is perceived by clients; (4) investigating the competition; and (5) conducting an internal assessment.

Stasiowski goes on to state that these five elements are common to all *Fortune* 500 companies. The strategic market-planning process provides the total framework of a contractor or design firm. The firm principals have a clear direction toward the vision and mission of the firm, the steps necessary to reach the goals, the objectives established, and a clear road map for the entire team within the organization.

Planning is critical and can help define your goals for the coming year—the structure, timetable, resources needed, and an action plan for the staff and the assignments for each. Without a plan, the marketing effort can wander aimlessly with much less productively than it would have otherwise. Develop your own plan with all your strategic planning tools. It will drive your company toward the opportunities that await, and you will avoid pitfalls. Where you choose to focus your efforts and your management philosophy will dictate how you should guide and train your staff. Keep in mind the following key aspects of this "risk versus opportunity" aspect of your plan.

You can't always eliminate all risk, because any business is a gamble, and all businesses incur risks. However, the following ideas may help you to reduce some of the risk:

- ♦ look out for threats
- ♦ reduce self-performed work (outsource more non-essential activities)
- ♦ schedule what needs to be accomplished during the year
- ♦ administer contracts diligently
- ♦ react aggressively to internal and external threats

To enhance opportunities:

- ♦ look internally for opportunities within your organization
- ♦ increase internal performance of activities that are your specialty
- ♦ plan to complete work by an established schedule
- ♦ manage your plan around completed work goals (results), building your record and reputation

The marketing plan should be considered your proactive approach to business. You should strive to think outside the box, anticipating the risks and opportunities on which you may be able to capitalize. The analogy that you are not marketing the quarter-inch drill bit, but in reality the quarter-inch hole, should be the underlying theme that should permeate your game plan. The plan must incorporate all available information about your firm, your advantages and disadvantages, and the strategy and reputation of your competitors.

Table 5.2 is a basic outline of a marketing plan and its different components. Every plan will have at least a summary, a SWOT, specific goals and objectives, strategies, and an action plan.

Having a summary with conclusions is self-evident, and yet many firms fail to put their full report into a readable summary that can be utilized to focus the effort throughout the year. The summary should reinforce the mission statement of the company and provide the background material of its purpose.

Component	Description
1. Table of contents	Listing of plan components.
2. Executive summary	Management summary of entire plan
3. Company strategic mission	Vision, goals, and strategies of company
4. SWOT analysis	Research and data analysis of internal and external market conditions garnered from media, private industry, government, associations, etc. Market forecasts/market share/trend assessment. Company resources (people, equipment, funding).
5. Marketing mix	Development of four Ps: product, price, promotion, place. Life cycle service/product strategies, previous sales history and future projections, client, prospects. Pricing issues. Promotional activities (marketing communications). Place-distribution challenges within market and target markets.
6. Strategic plan	Putting the above elements together for a cohesive plan, reviewing current resources for supplementing plan, developing a budget and tentative time frame.
7. Action plans	Goals and task assignment to achieve plan. Who, what, when where, and how, with costs and schedule to be monitored.
8. Controls and reviews	Regular reviews to update and adjust marketing plan.

Table 5.2. Marketing plan components.

Of special note is that investors and top management generally read no further than the executive summary, making this document even more critical to guarantee the financial support you will need to implement the full plan. If you are using outside financing to push your projects forward, bank officials will want to see your plan. In fact, they will insist on it. In addition to your plan, expect to be asked for financial statements, balance sheets, bank statements, tax returns, internal bookkeeping records, and more. But you can present all of your financial information and be rejected unless you present a business plan and a marketing plan. So consider your marketing plan and situational analysis not only a working guideline, but also a financial instrument.

Previously we examined the various components of research. This is one particular segment of the plan that needs sufficient time and attention to allow you to fully grasp the depth of the industry, its players, and the trends that will shape its future. You will need additional time, as well, to review the information you've obtained from industry publications, newspapers, magazines, newsletters, online sources, associations, government agencies, and private industry groups. All of these are excellent sources for viable business information. You should neglect none of these, particularly industry reports.

Goals and objectives provide the basis for what the company hopes to achieve from the marketing plan. This is really the meat and potatoes of the plan, which can be broken into various sub-plans for the company's future. Management is tuned to the sales plan you intend to influence through this marketing agenda, but there are several areas that will be affected by your advertising, marketing research, marketing collateral, training, technology, and PR plans. It is best that the goals and objectives set be as specific and measurable as possible. For example:

- position your company as a market leader or specialty niche player
- schedule development of the marketing plan
- create a realistic budget

Strategies and tactics are the procedures used by the company's marketing department to achieve the goals of the plan. What specific agenda will the company establish in order to achieve this plan?

Recommended actions (the action plan) are the heart of the plan. This is where the principals provide specific actions and outline the tasks to be performed, who will perform them, and when and how they will be performed.

Typical marketing plan

Let us now create a sample marketing plan. We won't go into mission statements here because we have already discussed them at length, but just remember they do not limit your freedom of choice in deciding where you are and where you plan to go. In many ways, they free you from having to consistently analyze the strategic decisions your company must face. Knowing what your business is, who your clients are, and what each of your customers values gives you and your team a clear direction to go in to obtain the corporate goals and objectives that radiate from your mission statement. Keep the mission statement in a long-term perspective to provide a purpose for your firm.

Let's use this worksheet. Create a list as follows:

1. Existing clients
2. Future clients
3. Market areas we currently work in and those we want to expand into
4. Products and/or services we provide
5. What are our financial objectives?
6. What skill do we particularly excel at?
7. What are the company's core values and beliefs?
8. What do we want to achieve for the employees of the company?
9. What image do we want to have established in the marketplace ten years from now?
10. Mission statement

Market size

You have unlimited access to statistical data on the market area. Forecasting the total size of your potential market, while also breaking it into specific segments (i.e., retail, commercial, government, private) should not be difficult. It will take some time and will require considerable analysis to make sure the information you have located is correct and will meet your needs. This research will be used throughout your marketing plan to help you make decisions about resource allocations in the pursuit of new business development. Don't depend on just what you uncover on the Internet or from the print media. Go out and talk with leaders in the market you want to enter. Talk with contractors, developers, owners, and economic development agencies to learn their thoughts. You can also supplement this process with telephone interviews and perhaps even some mail surveys. During your planning meeting you will be able to quote their view of the future, rather than your own, which will reinforce your thinking and build buy-in from your planning team. The following market-size questions may help you develop information about your market.

- What is the size of the market in land volume and dollars?
- What is the size of various market segments in land volume and dollars?
- How established (old) is this market?
- Is the market receptive to price fluctuation?
- Is the market receptive to outside fluctuations?
- Is this market cyclical? If so, can you determine the patterns and their cyclical sequences?
- How difficult is it to wrest market share away from the current industry leaders? Are there opportunities to penetrate this market despite the current dominant leaders in the (construction or other) industry?
- What unique skills, attitudes, and technologies are involved in the market?

This kind of planning is suitable for any service provider anywhere, but certainly more so for architects, engineers, construction people, landscape design, or any design professional service available.

Strengths and weaknesses

We reviewed earlier in this chapter the benefits of a SWOT analysis for your company and your market. This is a critical stage of the planning process when developing a situational analysis of the strengths, goals, opportunities, weaknesses, and assets of your firm.

This same review of competitors, using a SWOT analysis, will allow you to gather important information on each of them. One subcontractor has developed a computer competitor analysis sheet that reviews the results of each project it bids, documenting the bid results, the winner, the winner's bid, the winner's margin (against the contractor's own estimate), the winner's backlog, whether pre-construction services were provided, the number and names of competitors, the contractor's backlog at the time of bid, the customer relationship, and the anticipated start and end dates of the project.

This document also lists all the key project players, including the owner/developer, architect, engineer, and construction manager with an address, contact, and phone number for each. The project is described in depth with the building type, size based on gross square feet, the floors, what the structural system is, an arbitrary rating of the complexity of the project, and the delivery system. Added to this is an analysis of the design data: typical bay sizes, super live and dead loads, typical story height, seismic zone, lateral system, and other technological features the structure may contain. The company is then in a position to monitor the preferences, backlog, relationships, and intricacy of its competitor base and as such to control pricing and market planning. Your analysis may not go to this extreme, but remember, your competitor has the same tools available that you have, so it is best to try to obtain a good description of your strengths and weaknesses and those of your competitor as soon as you can.

Where are we today? Where do we want to be tomorrow?

This aspect of your plan is what you will eventually have to address. Many companies are so busy doing current work now, executing projects, putting out fires, and looking for new business opportunities that they neglect looking toward the future. It's hard to think about the day after tomorrow when you're so busy today that you can scarcely keep up. However, forecasting ten years into the future with key employees to help is an essential activity. During one of your early morning planning sessions, spend a bit of time writing a description of where you want the company to be ten years from now. Be as detailed as possible. What markets are you in, how many employees do you have, what market segments are you participating in, how are you perceived in the market, and how do your employees feel about the organization? This document then becomes the road map to your company's future.

The next part of the marketing plan will provide the objectives and actions to be taken to get the company to this destination.

Identifying prospects

Another important step of any marketing plan is determining who needs your services. Start with developing a list of who has been buying your services or product over the last five years. Break down this list of names into segments of the market in which they participate. Examples are commercial owners, government agencies, owner representatives, and the like. Then start to list the volume of work you have obtained from each. This should be further broken into base bid, extra and change orders, bid margins versus final executed margin, safety record, and a client maintenance factor.

Some clients demand an excessive amount of time with little or no payback in the form of new business. There is the tendency to develop a comfort level with these clients because we talk with them regularly, providing pricing and assisting with information requests. But they're tire kickers. They have no intention of buying but instead will pick your brain for information. Some of these clients can take up an inordinate amount of your time without adding significantly to your balance sheet. Get rid of them! You're too busy to be hand-holding!

The final step of this stage is to pinpoint your project locations.

The next stage involves developing a list of potential clients. Who are the people you'd like to do business with? Have you thought of new segments of the market, new territories, and clients with a good reputation for professionalism, fast payment of invoices, and low maintenance during the execution of the project? During your initial research, were there industry names that surfaced repeatedly?

Summarize your existing clients and the locations where you have performed their work. You need to examine actual results and strive to provide realistic guidance as to where you have had profitable results and where you have done a great deal of work but with marginal profits.

One of the most difficult aspects of this (or any) industry is eliminating work opportunities that exist but do not provide profit. Unless you have committed yourself to good causes, pro bono work, doing people favors, taking on jobs that don't allow you to cover even salaries, you need to think twice before taking on a project at cost. There is some justification to maintaining this type of backlog of work if it helps eliminate or absorb some of your fixed costs and overhead. However, many firms have been coerced into believing that a large backlog is the panacea for all of their problems, when in many instances, it only adds to the stress. Remember the 80/20 rule: Eighty percent of your profits usually come from 20 percent of your clients. Managing the other 80 percent is critical to your overall success.

During this activity, it is also important to analyze client needs as best you can. Basic to the review is how each client has rated each of the following aspects of your business: price, quality, service, location or convenience to his company's office, financial background, the training within your company, how your style or image meshes with his company's needs, exclusivity, product/service line, availability, warranty for services provided, ease to work with (evidenced by minimal change orders and back charges), knowledge of the market, reliability, and on-time delivery of the project as contracted. Being able to satisfy each specific client need is the difference between a contract and no contract. Price is important, but there are many important variables in the final decision.

Image

Here's the portion of the mission statement that should set the standard for all of your actions. What image do you want to give the marketplace, your clients, potential clients, and the A/E/C community in general? Marketing, as you will recall, is in large part a matter of perception. What perception do you want people to have about you? Besides the basics of being personally neat, clean, well groomed, prompt, courteous, friendly, cordial, and sincere, you are supposed to be a problem solver. We tend to forget that as problem solvers we perform as consultants to our clients and provide them with our ability, experience, and the resources we have at our disposal.

All firms today stress quality, within budget, on-time performance. Now, with that as the basic requirement, what does your company have to offer? This is the time to consider any niche opportunities you may have, special market segmentation aspects your company has, and special strengths. The James G. Davis Construction Company, in Rockville, MD, specializes in suburban office buildings and advertises widely that this is its specialty. The company conveys the idea that it is the building owner's "personal contractor." This firm goes out of its way to provide an environment that is a positive experience for the building owner. The philosophy and effort permeate all levels of the organization—from the secretary to the field forces. Whom do you think owners and their friends turn to first when they have another project to negotiate? Certainly someone who conveys that he cares about the project, takes a personal interest, and thus earns good marks from all his clients. "Oh, yes, we use Jim Davis exclusively. He takes care of our needs personally."

Qualifying prospects

There are hundreds of prospective customers in your markets. It is your job to determine the few who will provide you with the best opportunities. Deciding what is important and worthy of your company's time and attention will pay real dividends. The following questions must be included on the prequalification form you use for prospective clients and projects.

1. *Is this project real?* You can burn a lot of energy, time, and emotion on projects that are little more than pie-in-the-sky. Make sure the project has actually been scheduled and funded, and verify who is behind it. Don't let someone who has a reputation for fantasizing sell you on committing to a project when he hasn't yet talked to a bank, nailed down the specifics, signed all the paperwork, and set up all the participants.

2. *Does this project fit into your company mission and purpose?* This new project or client may seem exotic and have many good attributes, but if it does not meet the marketing mix you have established with your team members, then it should be shelved for the time being. If you don't have a schedule of upcoming business to keep your people busy and you need to keep them working, then you can, and probably should, consider that offbeat project—provided that your team is experienced enough with this type of work to do it properly.

3. *Where is the project located?* If this potential project falls outside of your current territory, it may require an unusual amount of resources to oversee its execution, and it may impose new risks.

4. *Who is the competition?* A review of who will be your anticipated competitors is important. Do any of your competitors have a personal relationship with the buying authority on this project? If it is a very close relationship, the project may be considered "wired"— actually closed to all other competitors.

5. *Will it be hard-bid or negotiated?* Will you have fifteen competitors or three? Will it be first cost or best final?

6. *Who will be the design team?* Some designers have a reputation for flair but lack the ability to assemble executable working documents. Will you be assuming additional risks?

7. *How will it be financed?* Will the financing be through bond issues, banks, or insurance companies? If you are to be a part of this project, you must know what the financial commitment and risks will be. If the project is not solidly financed, there's a chance you won't be paid.

8. *How big is the project?* Sometimes a project should be disqualified immediately due to its size, whether it be too large or too small. If the project is too large for your particular resources, consider joint venturing.

Action plans that generate strategies for follow-up

Now you have a list of potential clients and locations that have a profitable record. The most important stage of your marketing plan is the establishment of action plans. Planning is important, but every human endeavor needs a push to get it moving. Start with an overall strategy for translating your marketing plan into an action plan. Break the guiding plan into manageable pieces with competitive and promotional strategies, including timetables for each, and assign an individual to be responsible for the marketing plan (see **Table 5.3).**

Function	Activity	Responsibility	Due date	Done
SWOT analysis	Research	rdw	12/01/05	
Marketing mix development	Four P's analysis			
Strategic plan development	Assemble cohesive elements			
Action plans (to accomplish strategic plan)	Goal 1 Goal 2 Goal 3			
Controls	Review of plan activities			

Table 5.3. Marketing plan strategies.

This is the step in most marketing plans that will make or break it. Regular review of the status of the marketing strategies, with critical discussion of successes and failures, will assist with the redirection of your efforts. Accountability of individuals who are given responsibility is critical. These individuals will want to break down the action plan even further into manageable pieces. For example, if one of your strategies is to develop five new clients in the coming year, a subset of your plan will break down this objective as follows:

Meet with x, y, z potential clients in January

   ♦ Send letter of introduction with annual report, project profiles, etc.
   ♦ Follow-up call to be made one week later
   ♦ Follow-up visit within two weeks

- Obtain at least one new project from your initial effort
- Meet with a, b, c potential clients in February
- Continue the same sequence as January.

No plan works flawlessly. Every plan will need some modification because of unforeseen market conditions. A plan of action with a set timetable and individuals assigned who are accountable will get your company more quickly to its financial goals.

Persuasion, closing, and getting the order

Satisfying a client need and persuading that client that your proposal should be accepted is an art form in itself. Why should the client do business with you? Make a conscious effort to prepare a list of benefits that you will bring to the table when you meet with your client and discuss it thoroughly in advance with your entire team. Are you being selected on the basis of quality, speed, scheduling, financial strength, a friendly and competent staff, no "nickel and diming" during or after the construction process, value-engineering talent, or an ability to consistently bring the project in under budget? These are just a few of the aspects of persuasion that need to be fine-tuned and developed. An enormous amount of time and effort is expended to get to this stage. Having made such a huge investment, you now want to ensure that you will *close the sale and get the order.*

Encouraging your clients to close *now* is of paramount importance. Consistently probe the client for additional information. Establish the kind of rapport that will make it easy for him to tell you what you need to know. If you sense there are hidden agendas, hesitancy for any reason whatsoever, or something the prospective client isn't telling you, it's up to you to find out. Ask questions:

- How much do you want to pay?
- When do you want to start the project?
- We have two ways we can proceed. Which one would you prefer?

At the same time, you can add subtle items within your discussion that are integral to your proposal and that can trigger a need to close the deal. Perhaps you can add escalation terms to your proposal so your price will be increased or may not be applicable by a certain date. Create a verbal image of how the client will benefit when he signs on with you. Remind the client that time and profit will be lost by not acting in a timely manner. Yet you cannot press too hard, because then the client will become uneasy and may feel that *you* have a hidden agenda. Here's where you need to step carefully.

There is nothing illegal or unethical about these approaches. They are simply steps in moving a project from dead center to a line of action that your client will be making eventually. There are some people who cannot negotiate decisively. If your prospective client is one of those, you need to use your talent for persuasion to move him along. Your ability to get a final decision on projects can work toward the benefit of everyone involved.

Monitoring and making changes

Now you have completed your plan, individuals have been given their assignments, and have taken on the responsibility for tasks to be accomplished. Even more important now is the implementation of a series of checks and balances to monitor the plan and to establish the flexibility to make changes in course when road blacks are encountered. Contingency plans can be installed for "what if" scenarios based on resource and people problems as they occur. Schedules can be adjusted and regular feedback and discussion can correct activities that have pointed your effort in a direction contrary to the direction in which you wanted to go.

A marketing plan is just that—a plan. It is a dynamic tool rather than a document that is tossed on a dusty shelf. It must be regularly reviewed, analyzed, changed, and modified. It's a road map. As with any road map, you will encounter detours along the way, but your map should provide alternative options and flexibility for change. With the business world changing sometimes overnight, the traditional five-year plan can be an albatross. So, figure on a three-year plan to serve as an exceptional tool to ensure that all departments in your organization are on the same page. Each division of the company needs to provide feedback, allowing marketers to add their comments about budgeting modifications, human resource allocations, outside vendor assignments, and missed opportunities. Each time the marketing plan is reviewed or discussed, obstacles can be discussed and alternative solutions proposed.

The investment in marketing activities cannot be stressed too much. This is an outlay of financial and human resources that needs consistent assessment in the never-ending cycle of market planning and implementation. Controlling and accurately assessing the activities generated by the marketing plan are difficult and complex, but to be truly successful, they must be measured and monitored regularly. This effort will not be in vain. It will generate increased financial returns, and general goodwill and enhanced motivation for everyone.

Monitoring methods can be both qualitative and quantitative. A review of the strategic action plans with anticipated results compared to the overall operating statement of the company needs to be made and discussed. The marketing plan should be aligned with the financial objectives of the organization (sales, growth, return on investment, etc.) and should be tied in with the compensation for the marketing staff.

Now It's Time to Do It

A good motivational book written by Peter McWilliams, *Do It! Let's Get Off Our Butts*, is a good resource to peruse before you embark on your marketing plan. (It is out of print, but look for used copies on Amazon.com or Alibris.) There will be so many obstacles once you start down this road that it is helpful to read about them and develop confidence that you can overcome them.

With marketing an essential component of any A/E/C firm, the marketing plan and how you implement it is critical to your company's overall success. In order to develop commitment to the plan, you must communicate it with passion. Executives who neglect this essential component eventually will see their companies decline. As Peter Drucker has said, a plan is nothing "unless it generates work."

Chapter

6

Pre-construction Services and Promotion

Pre-construction is the act of getting involved with a potential client early to show how you would approach the solution of a complex problem from your perspective. This takes skill, keen ability, and insight.

Pre-construction represents one of the most frustrating aspects of business today. You can spend enormous time, resources, and considerable money developing detailed estimates for a client only to have the client take your information and peddle it to a competitor.

Pre-construction has become a large part of the manner in which we do business today. You are expected to help your potential client or support the assembled team by preparing drawings, schedules, personnel booklets, presentations, estimates, and proposals with limited guarantees of success. How you manage this portion of the bid process can provide you with additional profit every year.

Building Value through Promotional Methods

Pre-construction has evolved as one of the key professional tools for promotional activities in the building industry. If you are already a top-quality, first-class firm, why do you need to promote? Won't the industry come to you? It should, but the industry has no shortage of firms that are just as capable and proficient as yours is. Very few firms enjoy the luxury of having a lock on their segment of the market. Even if you should, most owners are required by their financial institutions to have at least three bidders on each project. Pre-construction can, however, give your company a considerable advantage by guaranteeing that your firm will be considered. It may also get you at least a "last look," which will give you the opportunity to decide whether you want to take the job or not (provided, of course, that it has been offered to you). This proactive approach to pre-construction services is a major component in the promotional tools successful companies use today.

A key element in marketing is the ability to promote your service so that it is perceived as the one that is best suited for a particular job. It is making sure that the decision-makers in your prospective clients' companies know about your firm, its capabilities, and experience, and that they have confidence and a sincere belief that yours is the right company for its new project.

In actuality, we are all promoters, whether it is of our companies or ourselves. We are consistently striving to make people aware of our unique capabilities. Whether you are an employee or an entrepreneur, you are marketing yourself to someone on a daily basis. Some people market themselves well. They look competent. They look professional. When they speak, they sound competent and professional.

When you are in business, either as owner, marketer, or project manager, someone has to promote the company and its services or products, or your competitor that *is* doing so will be recognized for *its* unique skill. If your competitor does it better than you do, who do you think will gain the competitive edge? Even if there is a designated marketer in your company, marketing is everyone's business. In the end, who wins? You may have the skills and expertise, but if you don't let people know, you will win no jobs.

One of the most certain methods to make your company a well-respected and sought-after member of a construction team is to prepare a detailed cost estimate for your portion of the project. Your company will develop a positive reputation by submitting estimated costs that are consistently on target.

Projects are analyzed initially for their financial worthiness. Your early cost advice and value engineering can be critical to allowing the project to start on a secure financial basis. Many preliminary decisions can influence whether a project moves ahead or is stopped in its tracks. Being known as a company that can help substantially at an early stage will make you a sought-after partner on the team. You should actively seek interaction with everyone involved with the assembly of the cost estimate to add valuable assistance, have an influence on the final outcome, and thus, you hope, develop an ongoing relationship. If you have a reputation as a company that can step in and help at any point, you may be called for particular projects at any time. Whatever the stage of the project—at its beginning, or at 30, 70, or 95 percent done—your estimating advice should be consistently available and updated as the project moves toward completion. A complete budget cost estimate allows a company to manage its own costs. An estimate that predicts the cost far in excess of actual bids results in mismanagement of owner's funds and can also cause an owner to suspend or postpone indefinitely a project that he has perceived as being too expensive. Utilizing professional cost estimating skills—whether it is in-house or by using a consultant—can be a prudent step to help the project team.

A concern of every firm owner is that the pre-construction services that the company has provided will be given to other members of the design team and that it will have expended its time and resources with no benefit to the company. This is always a potential problem. Diligent management of this activity, monitoring how you are being received and treated by your client, is important. It's difficult to accept, in this day and age, that one can't have complete confidence in clients or even joint venture partners. But to survive in the 21st century, one must be savvy, careful, intuitive, and watchful. Know what you are doing. Be aware of people's intentions, motives, and agendas. Be prepared for what might happen, and take whatever steps you need to in order to keep it from happening.

One firm prepares the estimates and drawings, and has photographs of the job site, but never lets any of them leave its control. The firm shares the information at group meetings, but refuses to turn any of it over to the project team until given a letter of intent or cash remuneration for the effort in which it has invested. If you don't believe you have the trust and confidence of the team at this stage, you may want to take your ideas to another team that may be more favorable to you.

You are not making these pre-construction cost estimates to benefit your competition or a project team who is obviously trying to take advantage of you. To stay out of situations like this, use your intuition and business sense. Here are some suggestions to help you.

1. *Go prospecting.* Seek new opportunities to demonstrate your abilities with cost estimates. When you hear about a job that comes in considerably over budget or about a project that is not moving ahead because the costs are so excessive, it should be music to your ears. This is your chance to approach principals of the firm and let them know how you would have done it. Make an offer to work with the company to find a solution to its problem. Very likely, at this point the frustration level is high and clients are open to any possibility that can make the project a reality.

2. *Never be late.* When an appointment has been made to present your budget proposal, *make sure you are on time.* The most damaging thing you can do once you've made an appointment is miss it altogether, or arrive late and not have the proposal ready for review as promised. The team you propose to work with is behind schedule already. So, your being late or unprepared tells these people that if you haven't met your first obligation, you are unlikely to meet any other. Fail at this juncture, and your modus operandi has been set in stone, at least with this client.

3. *Go the extra mile.* Always strive to set yourself apart from the competition by providing your clients with more than they ask for in services and end product. Many companies regularly prepare more than the basic budget bid. They present a schedule, with critical dates marked, their proposal bound in a three-ring binder with the company name and the title of the project on the cover, and a list of additional options available to save the client more time or money.

4. *Make flexibility and constant improvement your motto.* Make a consistent effort to improve your progress with pre-construction services by adding quality enhancements and standardizing various segments to speed up delivery time. Include new features to enhance your image of professionalism. Be on the leading edge of technology and be aware of future trends. If you do that, you will always have clients who will consistently pursue you because you make them look good.

5. *Develop partnerships.* Outsource as many tasks as you can. This allows you to take on more projects and to develop relationships with other teams of professionals who will help you achieve your goals while laying the groundwork for additional work. There are many excellent firms located near your company that can help with presentation packages, proposal writing, photography, scheduling, or any part of an estimate that is in their area of expertise.

6. *Keep learning about the competition.* Try to get a look at what the competition has done for your client in the past and what it proposes to do now.

7. *Ask for a performance review.* In addition, a follow-up interview with your client will give you a chance to ask how you did and what he would want done differently the next time. This will give you feedback to improve your performance, and will also allow the client to vent displeasure if there is something that did not go well. Performance reviews are essential. Without them, you'll never know if your client has a secret frustration.

8. *Maintain visibility in your specialty.* Let everyone know of your sincere desire to help with the pre-construction stage of projects for clients and potential clients. This can be done with a letter, on-line, through articles written for professional business publications or associations, or by word of mouth referrals.

9. *Use the Internet.* There are many exceptional web sites on which you can list your availability for pre-construction estimates, and perhaps even show what return on investment you have provided past clients with your efforts.

10. *Be available.* We must constantly be available to potential clients for pre-construction opportunities. When an estimate or help is needed, the need is usually immediate. Being easy to reach through e-mail, voice mail, or a pager is critical. You want to be the first person called because the client knows you can always be counted on for help.

Regarding this last suggestion, several companies have realized the opportunities that technology provides, allowing them to position their firms as outstandingly dedicated to customer service. Nowhere is this more evident than in the concept of a 24-hour-a-day service line. It doesn't necessarily mean that you will have your people working 24 hours a day. A combination of hot lines, toll-free numbers, pager systems, fax machines, and e-mail has opened a new field of service. There is now limitless access to information 24 hours a day from anywhere in the world. Thus, you and your clients can work on a computer from anywhere. Just make sure that there is at least one person in your office who can and will pick up messages on a regular basis and either direct them to the appropriate individual, or respond to them immediately. Utilize flextime for this purpose, and rotate your people so that no one feels unduly imposed upon.

The use of flextime gives your staff a great deal of versatility, and offers your clients comprehensive service. The use of a toll-free phone number is an outstanding investment, because no matter where your client or prospective client is located, he can leave messages and make requests, and you can control the time, place, and delivery of your response. You can utilize call forwarding to your cell phone, and you can utilize caller ID, to make sure you get your calls, and to know who is calling and whether you need to respond immediately. You may feel that these devices—pager, cell phone, e-mail, toll-free number—will give you no peace, but the business environment today is rife with emergency situations, and if you want to be competitive with people who have such services, you must, too. Check your voicemail and e-mail daily. It's a courtesy you can't afford to ignore.

Turn cold calls into warm calls

"Hello, Tom. Long time no see! I hear your local baseball team is killing the competition. The next time I'm in your area, how about getting some tickets? I wouldn't mind having a hot dog with you."

If you are an outgoing friendly person, you find it easy to talk with anyone anywhere. That kind of person can sit down next to someone on an airplane or bus, and in ten minutes can find out what he does, if he's married, how many kids he has, where he went to school, and where his favorite restaurant is. It's a strange thing. Without asking, you can easily figure out every human being's favorite subject. Himself. Most people get very little opportunity to express themselves to others. The wife doesn't listen. The kids don't care. Co-workers aren't the slightest bit interested, and strangers on the street will think you're nuts if you tell them you just ate the most fabulous hamburger, or saw an incredible sunset or were teary-eyed at a movie. But there are people who will listen to you, if you first express an interest in them and let them talk to you *about themselves.* Learn to be a terrific listener. Don't break in. Let the other person talk himself out, something he never gets a chance to do. Be interested.

What's this about? This is about the fact that a necessary element in the A/E/C industry is making *cold calls!*

No one is fond of cold calls, but this one strategy, hated as it is, can make a significant difference in your business. We are all nervous about making these calls because there's always the risk of rejection. The problem with ignoring this activity is the loss of potential new business opportunities, and most definitely, new friends. Often on cold calls, you will meet congenial, friendly people who are willing to learn more about your company. They are usually in much the same situation you are in. They need new work. They need to keep their projects within tight budgetary constraints, meeting aggressive schedules, managing ongoing changes to documents, and coordinating a multiplicity of relationships in the field, office, and with their clients. So, as busy as the prospect is, if you can get him to sit down and talk with you, and you let him pour out his frustrations to you, you will have made a friend, and you hope, a client.

However, the old cold calls we used to make, dropping in without an appointment or any knowledge of the companies we are calling upon, rarely work today. To turn a cold call into a warm one, you need to analyze and plan by first deciding which companies could really benefit from your services. You must have a marketing strategy to provide an ongoing program of services for them, you need to make an effort to get them to understand you, your company, the benefits you offer, and the fact that they can depend on you to reliably perform for them. But more important, you need to learn who the people are in the company, as much as you can about their background, the kind of work they do, what projects they have done, and any tidbits of information you can learn about the key principals. Brainstorm with your staff, friends, colleagues, wives, cousins, and so on. And, of course, check the Internet.

Pick a firm. Send the CEO a letter. Tell him who you are. Tell him what you do. Offer some pro bono service as an introduction. Offer to partner with the company at some future date. Suggest that an alliance with your firm will be an advantage to his firm. Ask about problems the firm is dealing with currently. Mention problems you have solved for others. Mention organizations to which you belong. Suggest meeting for lunch. Find out what organizations this person is involved in and where he is active. Accidentally running into him at a chamber of commerce meeting would be an ideal time to meet him face to face and make a connection. If he volunteers at a homeless shelter, you volunteer there, too. If he belongs to a country club, you join it, too. If his wife and your wife use the same hairdresser … You get the picture, don't you?

Follow up with other types of mailings—brochures, postcards. When you have completed a project and have developed some literature on it, use that literature to follow up on these contacts.

Desktop publishing software allows you to produce high-quality pieces of research to keep your perspective clients apprised of new trends and information about your segment of the industry. This material can be sent by mail, fax, or e-mail in the form of a newsletter. Include case histories of some of your success stories.

Now, it's possible that these appeals will fall on deaf ears. It's possible that your brochures, postcards, and newsletters will hit the round file. People are busy. They often don't have time to read. Sometimes, these things land in a basket, and are eventually buried under a ton of similar materials. But, now you make an effort to reach that prospect by phone. Offer lunch.

"Ya gotta eat, Tom. Meet me for a bite at the Gorilla Grille. We can talk about baseball, if you prefer. But I'd really like an opportunity to tell you what XYZ Design Group can do for your company."

These warm calls will be an opportunity for you to learn more about your potential clients. In these meetings, you can discuss their needs and what problems they have that you may be able to satisfy. Engage them in "value conversations" that ask probing questions to uncover what keeps them awake at night. Expand this technique to others in the organization with whom you may have come into contact, whether it is in the field, in the accounting department, or at the front desk. Once the personnel in a company know you as a problem solver and not an order taker, you will see a change in attitude and you may gain a new client.

Niche marketing

Niche marketing can be your answer to carving out a successful business in the general A/E/C industry, and perhaps redirecting part or all of your business toward specific areas of expertise. This follows the logic that most clients would prefer to hire companies that specialize in their area of need. Clients today cannot afford to pay a firm to "go to school" on their project. They seek out companies that have exceptional knowledge of or a proven record in the type of work they need. Niche marketing also allows you to focus your attention away from just trying to maintain volume and toward increasing profits. Most clients are willing to pay a slightly higher fee to a company that has related experience because they know it will save them the time and aggravation of dealing with work that is performed poorly because it is not the provider's first or best area of expertise. So, how do you discover your niche?

- Survey your clients and potential clients to learn what needs aren't currently being adequately served.
- Keep abreast of trends in the industry by attending industry functions, reading industry publications as well as general business news, and noting articles by industry experts on future trends.
- Be creative.

♦ Decide for yourself where your market's needs will be in the future and develop your expertise in those areas.

Once you have established a niche, how do you take advantage of it? Promote yourself as an expert. The best way for you to become known in a niche market is to be recognized as the leader in your area of expertise. Here are some suggestions.

1. *Publish.* Develop a half-dozen outlines for stories that might be of interest to prospective clients—stories that give practical advice and not ones that boast about how great your firm is—and submit them to the publications your clients read. Also, send press releases to those publications about new projects, new hires, completed projects, or anything that happens in your firm that might be considered news. The more often people see your name in print, the busier and more successful they will know you to be.

2. *Teach.* There is no better or more useful way to establish credibility in your field than teaching, particularly when you are able to teach prospective clients. Look into opportunities to make presentations at seminars given by associations to which your clients belong. They are always interested in finding new speakers. (If you are not an experienced speaker, take some public speaking courses at your local college, or join Toastmasters. You know what a dynamic speaker is like; here's your chance to become one.)

3. *Be visible.* When you attend functions sponsored by organizations to which your clients belong, walk around, say hello to people, hand out your business card.

4. *Promote.* Highly targeted promotional efforts, like direct mail, advertising, and media publicity, are far more effective and cost efficient than promoting the broad, diversified services of a firm to a general audience. (Check out the SMPS publications *Tell the World: Results-Oriented Public Relations*, by Dianne Ludman Frank; *The Fame Game: Crafting the "Expert" Article*, by Carl Friesen; and *Principles for Principals*, by Joan Capelin. All of these will give you superb information on how to get your name in the news and how to be seen as an expert in your field.)

To survive in the years ahead as the niche markets you develop become increasingly crowded, you will need to develop and refine two skills: (1) effective use of a database to ensure that you are communicating to all possible prospects, and (2) flexibility to ensure that you can always stay ahead of the curve.

Remember that today's niche may become tomorrow's overcrowded market. If you do a good job of becoming well known in your field, you should be able to stay at the top of your niche even during tough times. Nevertheless, it would be wise to employ the same creativity you use to uncover today's niche to find other profitable niche markets to explore in the future.

Awards programs

These programs, which have proliferated around the country, are an ideal way for you to gain recognition and respect in the market. Regardless of what award you may win, it is important to invite your clients to the recognition dinner as a further method for networking and identifying your efforts. The awards you receive should be displayed in your reception area to highlight your achievements. Prospective and existing clients alike will see your awards and recognize the respect our company has received from the industry. Don't stop here; this is an ideal time to publish press releases or articles describing the attributes that your firm utilized to achieve this award. Obtain reprints of anything published and distribute them to all existing and potential clients. Present a framed copy of these awards to your client. He may even be so delighted to be associated with a winner, he may hang it in *his* office. Include a photo of the individuals responsible to illustrate the teamwork that exists between your organization and your clients (even a group shot at an awards dinner can be of value).

Seminars and workshops

A perfect way to educate and influence a group of people is to hold seminars or workshops with a focus on their learning something new, during which you have the opportunity to explain the benefits of your product or services. These sessions can be conducted at trade shows, in conjunction with professional associations, industry groups, universities, or at a potential customer's office during the lunch hour. The "box-lunch" concept provides a tremendous opportunity for you to take your message in-house to your targeted audience. Over lunch, clients can conveniently listen to your presentation on how you can help them do their job better, faster, or more cost-effectively.

Think about continuing education credits, which are available for professionals. If you can expand your educational opportunity to meet the criteria that continuing education associations have set, and work with them to set up courses under your sponsorship, you can then assist clients in meeting their educational goals.

Check out the American Association for Adult and Continuing Education (www.aaace.org) and the International Association of Continuing Education and Training (www.iacet.org) to learn how you can offer CEUs to attendees. If you do this on a regular basis, you may be devoting time and people to this endeavor, but you will have created a niche market for yourself, and the opportunity to meet a great many people in the industry to whom your name may have meant nothing heretofore. As you continue to offer educational services, you will be bringing more business to your company because you've become a well-known and trusted colleague.

Technology has made it possible for workshops to be PowerPoint extravaganzas with links today to web sites, job-site cameras for "real time" viewing of project locations, or teleconferencing capabilities so that several members of your organization can participate from various national and international locations. Combined with this is the chance to distribute additional information about your company, your employees, your unique benefits, articles written about you, and testimonials.

These public-speaking opportunities, whether for a seminar or before industry groups, can be highly beneficial. A notice, including copies of media coverage, can be sent to your prospective target audience alerting it to your upcoming speaking engagement. You can also extend personal invitations to those whom you want in that audience.

This same format will work in your own organization to position you as a leader and provide you with a forum. Helping to mentor and lead training programs for new recruits can position you as a concerned, knowledgeable leader. This effort will also help develop a close relationship with your team, and will enhance your reputation.

Volunteer to help direct in-house planning programs. Use these programs to express your ideas and the positive direction in which you want to help move the company. Sally Handley, former partner in The Marketing Partnership, of Kinnelon, NJ, says: "We believe an educated client is our best customer, so we offer seminars describing roofing, curtain wall and mechanical/electrical systems, their inherent problems, and our unique approach to solving those problems. We believe that this (promotional tool) distinguishes us in our very competitive market, simultaneously communicating the specialized services we provide."

Writing for success

There are many publications such as daily newspapers, weekly business journals, monthly magazines, and association newsletters that are looking for knowledgeable building industry experts who can write and comment on the industry. You, better than anyone else, have a good understanding of your specific segment of the industry and of the latest trends and indicators. There exists an opportunity to share that information with both print and electronic media. This can take the shape of press releases announcing changes or new work your company has acquired, or alerting the industry about new market audits or surveys that you have commissioned.

Another option is to regularly write articles and editorials. This develops credibility for both you and your company and helps support the industry. You will also gain recognition and respect from your peers and potential clients, placing you a step ahead of your competition.

The right kind of communication program helps position your company in the marketplace and lets the public in on your special niche, to learn about your recent successes, what your clients are saying about you, and how you were able to bring that last project in under schedule and within budget. Excellent communication skills can place you at the top of the industry overnight.

Whenever something written by a member of your staff appears anywhere, distribute copies to all of your clients and contacts. Share your recent column about saving money or enhancing productivity. This illustrates your ingenuity, innovation, and support of the industry. It will enhance your reputation of leadership and authority, and shows that yours is the kind of firm people want to contact when there is a problem. As we all know, this is one business that has plenty of problems to be solved. Who better for them to turn to than the industry expert?

Demonstrations and field trips

Demonstrations and field trips in the industry have recently gained in popularity. They represent another way to bring your target audience to you. There are many opportunities for you to arrange field trips to your job site with the help of subcontractors and vendors, with student groups, or association events. These events must be organized, planned, and rehearsed. It takes considerable time to prepare an environment where all of the pieces flow together. Don't hesitate to invite the local media. They're always interested in something new and different. A field trip to explore a high-rise in the making, or, wherever it poses no danger, to have a demonstration of a large piece of construction equipment will provide an educational opportunity for middle school students, perhaps, and provide some interesting and unusual media coverage.

Kling-Linquist, a national design firm in Philadelphia with expertise in designing a full range of office, computer, research, and manufacturing facilities for both the public and private sectors, has large conference rooms it allows industry groups to utilize on a regular basis, bringing a broad mix of the market into its office for exposure and networking. The firm's name is on every promotional piece, the industry groups appreciate this courtesy, and the exposure for the company is extensive.

Trade shows, exhibits, and displays

Trade shows are scheduled in every city in the United States, and everywhere else as well. They've become a huge industry, but one needs to be analytical to work out whether it's financially feasible to hold them, or be a part of them. They need to be cautiously managed due to the extensive costs and staff requirements needed to make them successful. They can also be a tremendous source of visibility for your company and can provide you with numerous leads for new projects and contacts. Some firms have built their entire marketing effort around the aggressive working of trade shows where they know their clients will be present.

Teleconferences

Teleconferences have changed the way we view the market for our companies and how we manage our efforts. Teleconferencing allows us to address multiple audiences in several cities, answer multiple questions, and do it all from our offices. At the same time, we can have our clients actually take an electronic walk through a proposed project, making changes and modifications as they go.

Company web sites

A web site is indeed a window to the world. However, many sites are static, uninteresting, tedious, repetitive, and trite. When you browse, notice how many are exactly alike. But for the name of the firm, and the color selected, you might be looking at the same site repeatedly.

When creating your web pages, design the content to appeal to the decision-makers of the companies you wish to pursue.

- Make a list of the people you are interested in as clients. Make sure that each of these is, in fact, a decision-maker.
- Decide what the decision-maker needs to know in order to decide to use your services.
- Analyze how the competition handles their promotions to decision-makers.
- Identify the "real" market needs.
- Design your site to reflect the fulfillment of those needs.

Establishing Networking Goals

Networking is the secret to making the contacts every businessperson needs in order to be successful. Have you ever attended a function, or a political rally, at which the key person was able to address great numbers of people by their first names? This person has charisma, most certainly; a phenomenal memory, most surely. But more important, this person has a networking system and he or she works at it systematically and all the time.

Networking can be done casually or randomly, or as one author once suggested, managed and recorded as one would record sales, with consistent follow-up and a planned strategy. But it must be done, for without this strategy, any marketing or promotion you do is wasted, unless you reach out and network to a large number of people. Networking is a numbers game. The more people you reach or talk to, the more opportunities you will have for being remembered, and being contacted for business.

When networking becomes prospecting

Make a list of 12 to 15 possible clients that could generate business for you. Look at these possibilities: financial organizations, boards of directors, presidents of companies, highway commissions, city council, owners, contractors, property owners, architects, engineers, county board, etc. Research these companies or organizations thoroughly through Dun & Bradstreet reports, company reports and newsletters, interviews with other companies that interact with them, and even Internet archives. Find out what they like to do, who makes their decisions, and what their long-range goals are. Are they active with certain professional societies or civic organizations? Do they regularly attend industry functions? Target the individuals who are the decision-makers for your service and ask questions about what they like and don't like, and about their personal backgrounds. Now you are ready to start networking, armed with statistics and information that will make the experience much more positive and rewarding for everyone. But don't expect instant results, because networking is an ongoing process. Generally, it can take five or six meetings before a person feels comfortable with a new person.

Lead gathering: prospect and qualify

You need to be exposed to many individuals before you meet the client who will provide you with new business or leads. To be effective, this networking program must be documented. Write down in a notebook, journal, or on your computer whom you met, where you met him (her), what was said, what suggestions were made, and what agreements were made. If you get an opportunity to make an appointment with that person, review this record. He or she will be impressed with your marvelous memory when you recall details of the previous meeting. But more important than that, you are establishing a new relationship, and your recollection of past discussions will prove that this is important to you. The record will also help provide you with clues as to how you can help this person and his firm, and also, what value he can add to your networking arsenal. If you are adding a new friend to your circle in the hope that he or she will provide you with leads to friends, don't think for a moment that your new friend isn't doing the same thing!

Not all contacts will provide you with orders for new business, but each individual you come into contact with can become part of your sphere of influence within your broad network. A contact may know someone who can open a closed door, make an introduction, or provide a productive lead. You will find that it generally takes 25 contacts to result in five qualified leads, which eventually will develop into two orders for your company. This is a considerable amount of work for two projects, but the benefits of volume contacts through networking can accelerate this process for you and enhance your bottom line.

(Don't forget, two projects can yield business worth thousands of dollars, or millions of dollars, or hundreds of millions of dollars. So don't let the number "two" daunt you.) Like ripples in a pond, every contact may have a delayed or far-flung reaction.

Working the market

Attending industry functions and belonging to professional societies are good things to do, but without action on your part, these activities will not materialize into meaningful results. Before you attend any function, you should consider what you want to accomplish, whom you would like to meet, and what result you hope to get from these contacts. Briefly, consider the questions you would like to ask in order to start a dialogue because it will make it much easier to focus on the individual's responses without worrying about what to say or do. You may even want to use these functions as an opportunity to announce some new achievement or direction your company has taken. Any time someone asks, "How's it going?" you should be prepared to present an enthusiastic and interesting reply, touting that grand achievement!

Professional societies and local industry groups can provide a wealth of beneficial experiences for you to tap into. However, you need to spend the time to become involved with committees and take leadership roles, if you plan to maximize the contacts you make. What better way to show what you know, or how you can help, than by working with a person whose company you'd like to cultivate?

Make yourself known as an individual who gives more than he takes. The old saying "always do more than you are asked to do" is good advice in the critical area of networking. We all have many chances to make a difference. We can do the minimum necessary, or we can go out of our way to do a little bit more, and the other person will walk away from the contact saying, "Wow! What a team player!" or "He seems genuinely concerned about me and my problems."

Author and lecturer Zig Ziglar, who wrote *5 Steps To Successful Selling,* among others, said it best: "You get whatever you want if you help enough people get whatever they want." That's not a bad motto to live by.

Review your networking goals: Make at least two calls a day. Networking is an ongoing endeavor. We need to constantly examine ways to expand our networks, both personally and professionally. The first basic step is to stay in touch with your past contacts. Phone calls, notes, clippings from newspapers slipped into an envelope, with a scrawled note, "Bill, this seems right down your alley. Arch", or even a recent newsletter you received in the mail can accomplish this. Regularly updating your Rolodex and computer database with promotions, moves, and family changes is vital. Keep track of what your friends and colleagues are doing. Next, you need to look for new avenues of networking opportunities. Try to attend groundbreakings, advance project meetings, press gatherings, and industry social events, and keep the cold calls rolling. Try to maintain your contact levels at the two new calls a day you promised yourself to make to people not included in your database. This small step alone will add 500 new contacts a year to your Rolodex, and most certainly a few dollars to your bottom line.

Also, keep in mind the need to expand your own personal network for career stability and exposure. No individual in the world is "set for life." Conditions change, and you may have the need to move on. Eighty percent of new employment opportunities come from unlisted sources. What better opportunity to keep yourself plugged into the market than by maintaining a network to help you improve your career? Those who find themselves in the unemployment rolls traditionally spend one month for each $10,000 of their salary base while looking for a new job. Thus, if you're in the $50,000 bracket, expect to be searching for five months; and if you're at the $120,000 bracket, you'll probably be out of work for a year. Contacts, either personal ones or previous professional contacts, are what will make the difference for you.

Build your reputation as a leader (add value to bring in value)

We live today in a value-conscious society. Quality and value are not an option, they are a given. Each of your networking opportunities must focus on bringing value and real worth to the relationship with a long-term perspective. Not only will this enhance the quality of relationships, but the results will ultimately pay greater dividends to your company, and thus to you.

Make customers and clients your friends. Networking is an exceptional way to expand your circle of friends, support, resources, contacts, and that valuable grapevine through which you receive important information. The friendships you ultimately establish are by far the most rewarding and fun. Each new contact you make has the potential of developing into a lifetime friendship. We all need friends—people who will share our ideas, thoughts, and problems; people who will help us sort through the masses of information forced upon us daily. Our workdays are becoming longer, stress levels higher. What better way to improve the quality of the workday than working with people who are friends? Nine times out of ten, these are the people who will provide your next contract, without the usual hassles. It takes just a handful of these good friends to make the job you are doing more enjoyable, and more gratifying.

A Positive Attitude

Many people, from Zig Ziglar to Dale Carnegie—author of *How to Win Friends and Influence People,* a book that has been a guideline worldwide for more than 50 years—have written about the merits and significant benefits of a positive mental attitude. Why then, do so many people refuse to believe the physiological advantage you can achieve for yourself and everyone in your company by maintaining a positive attitude? Every task you undertake will be easier and better if you put a positive spin on it. A positive mental attitude is simply allowing your subconscious to consider what you want as the final outcome of your work. By concentrating on a successful outcome, addressing the problems, and working out potential solutions and scenarios to overcome any difficulties, you will eventually achieve success.

It is said that Thomas Edison made suffered more than 1,000 unsuccessful attempts to develop the light bulb before he finally succeeded. Maintaining a positive attitude throughout a series of failures provides the inner strength you need to overcome exterior environmental conditions and uncooperative individuals you will encounter along the journey to success. Negative people do not succeed. Positive people always do.

Follow Up! Follow Up! Follow Up!

Meeting hundreds of new people through networking is a good thing, but unless you follow up promptly, your efforts will come to nothing, and you've wasted your time. A personal note, a company brochure, an article regarding something that was discussed, a brief phone call are all excellent ways to ensure that you will be remembered. If you don't follow up, and you run into the same person six months later, you may say, *"Hello, Ms. Jenkins. We met at the AIA conference in June. How are you?"* Ms. Jenkins will look at you blankly, because she won't remember!

As mentioned, it normally takes five or six meetings to develop a relationship. A follow-up can accelerate this process if you do it promptly, with professionalism, and political correctness. Get a business card. Then you'll have the correct spelling of names and addresses. Write everything you can remember about this person on the back of the card, with the date of the meeting; then file the card! (You can, if you want to, load this information into a database.) This growing database can be the basis of leads, information gathering, peer network, associations, companies, possibility of future work opportunities, and market niches.

Jack Miller, a Houston, TX, civil engineer and owner of a seminar business, has done everything in the construction business, including marketing. One noted construction writer has dubbed him "the living legend with mud on his boots." In May 2001, the Construction Writers Association presented him with its highest honor, the Silver Hard Hat Award, for a lifetime contribution to the construction industry.

As the world's number-one authority on achieving success in construction, Miller's seminars draw construction professionals from across the United States and Canada. He consistently preaches the merits of getting in front of clients and potential clients as often as possible. Do it with a phone call, newsletter, cold calls, or notes. These regular communication efforts may provide the opportunity to get in on the ground floor with a new project or hear about some other beneficial tidbit that could help you grow your business.

Monthly Reports

Reporting to your executives, your peers, or your staff is essential. Do it on a regular basis. First, it lets them know what you are doing. Second, it suggests ideas to them so they can help you. Third, it triggers the idea that information they have might be useful to you and move your efforts along. Make it a habit to maintain some kind of journal of activity. Use your computer. Try to do it daily. Write the date, list whom you saw, what they said, and what you think the prospect for a project might be. If there was any suggestion for a follow-up, then do it. Not only should you use this information for a monthly report to your executives and your staff, but also you should review what you wrote two weeks or a month prior so you know with whom to follow up. If you don't have time for anything more, use e-mail.

Following a meeting at a luncheon, perhaps you can write as follows: "Hello, Jack. It was great getting together with you at the XYZ luncheon. How about meeting for lunch next week? What you told me piqued my interest, and I may have a few suggestions to help you."

Later: *"Hi, Jack. How's it going? Did you ever follow up on that name I gave you? How did that work out? Let me know."*

That's the benefit of writing things down, and providing for others a monthly report.

No one knows what you have done over the last month better than you do. A monthly report will keep this process manageable and should draw on problem areas during the year rather than only once a year. Some companies have broken their monthly reports down to four key topics: accomplishments, problems, opportunities, and outlook (APOOs).

Networking is a considerable amount of work. Do we really need to take on more work with the limited time that we have? Is it worth it? The most successful people in America, and in fact, the most successful people in the world, will tell you "yes." Nothing is worth more.

Chapter

7

Marketing and
Sales Technology

If you look back at the construction industry over the past 25 years, you will observe that not much has changed in the way a building is built. A revolution has taken place, however, in the office. And the revolutionaries are the marketers.

The world of the marketer in the construction industry has changed dramatically. Contact names have moved from Rolodex files to electronic databases. Research is seldom conducted at the library, but rather on the Internet. Marketing materials are often not created on paper. Photographs are rarely stored as prints. Communication is no longer solely the domain of the telephone. And presentations are no longer made using charts and overheads.

Technology has touched almost every aspect of the marketer's job, except the most important part—the ability to understand a prospect's needs and explain how the marketer's company is best qualified to satisfy the prospect. Otherwise, it's a whole new world.

Four areas of technology—the Internet, digital cameras, presentation tools, and communication devices—are responsible for most of the changes that affect marketing professionals.

Now, more than ever, marketers can learn a tremendous amount about industry trends, prospects, and competitors; organize vast amounts of data on prospects and clients; chronicle all kinds of job site activity; and give dynamic presentations, using affordable, easy-to-use hardware and software.

The Internet

The Internet has revolutionized the way marketing professionals collect information and promote their services.

E-mail has enabled us all to communicate more efficiently with one another, and professionals to communicate with prospects, clients, fellow employees, and project team members. It also provides the means to send files and information, have it edited or revised, and sent back. Most importantly, you can send information and documents to your clients for approval and save a lot of time compared to other means.

The Internet has become a vast network of data about markets, competitors, and prospects, giving professionals an edge over competitors who aren't connected. Moreover, professional web sites allow you to present information about your company to prospects and potential employees.

Digital Cameras

Digital cameras have become the tool of choice for everyone in America. Pictures, instead of being printed, are being saved electronically, and thus can be transmitted by e-mail. The cost is affordable, considering the value; the results are outstanding; and as a means of sending information to clients and others, there is no better way to convey the value of what you can do to help a client than by showing him what you have done in the past, suggesting that you can do the same or more for him.

Digital cameras have numerous applications for the construction marketer. Although they are a fairly expensive investment, they can save considerably on the cost of photo development and image scanning. One option found with some digital cameras is a swivel lens and software that allows you to create panoramic images of job sites.

Video cameras also are being installed on the job site to monitor job progress. The cameras are linked to a dedicated server run by the company, and images from them can be viewed on the company's web site. Some of the higher-end cameras are mounted on swivel mounts. Several people can simultaneously manipulate the camera, and thus the view, by moving the mouse from side to side or up and down. These job-site video cameras serve as important marketing tools and provide the professional or owner with remote access to important job-site functions such as material delivery and the numbers of people working on specific trades.

Presentation Tools

If you're still using overhead and slide projectors and your old easel, perhaps you should put them in storage as backup for a better technology. Your ability to level the playing field with larger competitors has been greatly enhanced by the presentation tools available today.

PowerPoint

One of the most popular software tools today is Microsoft PowerPoint. With its substantial R&D support and compatibility with so many complementary software programs, it offers a great deal of flexibility and ease of use.

PowerPoint is a *presentation graphics program,* software with which you can create a slide show. PowerPoint helps you generate and organize ideas, and provides tools to create charts, graphs, bulleted lists, text, multimedia video, animation, and sound clips. It also assists you in creating slide show supplements such as handouts, speaker's notes, and transparencies.

PowerPoint provides you with dozens of templates for your content, and also includes a step-by-step wizard to generate your own format. You can create, with desktop graphics software, a custom background incorporating your company's logo and other visual elements. Also, the Microsoft web site includes a PowerPoint area (www.microsoft.com/powerpoint) where you can learn more about the software and download clip art, textures, sounds, and animations.

The program allows users to tailor one presentation to multiple audiences with an option called *Custom Shows*. It creates different versions of your presentation in one master file, so you show only the slides you need for each audience. With *Pack And Go*, which assembles and compresses all the files you need onto floppy disks, you can easily travel with your presentations.

PowerPoint also allows you to publish and view PowerPoint animations and presentations on your web pages. You can take advantage of the enhanced animation, hyperlinks, special effects, and built-in sound functions to build animated web pages that stand out from static HTML web pages. So when you want to make a professional presentation to a prospect from a remote location, the prospect can log onto your web site and view a complete PowerPoint show.

PowerPoint Viewer enables PowerPoint users to share their presentations with people who do not have PowerPoint installed on their computers.

With practice, you should be able to quickly put together professional presentations. And if you want to accelerate the process, most major colleges and

technical schools now offer presentation design classes, as do private organizations. You can usually find them listed on the Internet under "presentation training."

Projectors

Most marketers today prepare their presentations on a desktop PC and save them to a laptop or notebook computer to transport to presentations. Notebook computers give mobile salespeople all the comforts of a desktop computer: processing power, high-resolution graphics displays, and multimedia features. These systems are a good way to take product demonstrations or colorful presentations into clients' offices, provided you have some means of displaying the computer's images. Unless all your clients have equipped their conference rooms with projectors, you could be placed in the position of asking a group of people to gather around the small screen of a portable PC.

That's why a portable LCD projector is a necessary companion for a notebook computer. Although the quality of a projected image cannot quite match the best fixed-projection systems, portable projectors are usually able to display clear screen images in moderately large rooms, even with some lights on to allow conversation and eye contact.

Projectors are easy to use. Better ones have a single-cable connection to the computer you're using. Software to run the projector must be installed in your computer. Once it is turned on and connected, it's simply a matter of making the presentation.

There are several factors to consider when purchasing a projector:

1. *Brightness*. Lamp brightness is measured in the ANSI standard unit lumens. Projectors of 140 to 250 lumens with halogen lamps handle a 10-foot screen in a moderately lit room (enough light to easily read a newspaper), 300 lumens of halogen or 250 of metal halide lamp projectors can handle 6-foot screens in bright rooms or possibly be acceptable for up to 20-foot diagonal screens in darkened rooms, and 350 to 500 lumens of metal halide driven projectors are comfortable on 25- (350 lumens) to 30-foot screens in darkened rooms. They can handle virtually any lighting up to 10-foot screens.

2. *Image clarity*. Most projectors provide 800 x 600 SVGA capability, consistent with most laptop computers, and some provide true 1024 x 768 resolution. Older, and typically less expensive, PC display systems that only support VGA resolution impose a strict functional limitation because they blank out when users attempt to display images configured for greater than 640 x 480.

3. *Portability*. If you go to a client's office with your notebook and a briefcase, you want your projector to be as lightweight as possible. Most of the best projectors are less than 20 pounds, and some are small enough to fit in your briefcase. If you travel, you'll either need a super-lightweight one (less than 10 pounds) or a rolling case (wheels and extension handle) that is small enough to be standard carry-on luggage.

Communication Devices

Moving computers from the desktop into the field has been the ultimate dream of every person in sales and marketing. This dream is being realized on many fronts. We all know you can make or break a job in the field, not in the office.

Communication between office and field will never be the same again. You may believe that this has no direct application to marketing or sales. But the truth is, it has *everything* to do with marketing and sales. The ultimate goal is to have a satisfied client that provides repeat business. What is better than working with a client who is thoroughly impressed with your capabilities, happy with the successful project you have just completed, and willing to tell others of your ability and technical expertise?

Virtual-reality models and CD-ROMs

Virtual reality models and CD-ROMs have changed the way we market and sell our ideas. Today, it is possible to provide clients with a virtual walk-through of your ideas for designing and building the next project. Sitting down in your client's office and providing a step-by-step discussion of its concept can give you a dynamic advantage in today's competitive marketplace, where price alone traditionally has dictated the final outcome. A virtual walk-through can provide an interactive, real-time marketing tool that lets you make changes to the electronic image as the client expresses an opinion on what is being shown. After the presentation is complete, you have a vision based on *client input, client need, and client desire.* You now have a true blueprint of what the client wants, a guideline to follow from beginning to end.

CD-ROM brochures

Digital cameras and the proliferation of CD-ROM recording hardware have made the development of CD-ROM brochures for marketing a reality. These tools make a sensational presentation that can produce a three-dimensional, virtual-reality view of your people, your projects, and testimonies from happy clients. These CDs can be mass-produced and distributed to potential clients. The ability to instantly hook up to your web site can be incorporated into the disk. These disks should be left with the prospect for additional review. They are also excellent for use at trade shows and as promotional mailers.

Voice recognition technology

Voice recognition technology offers considerable opportunities for the industry. The development of voice recognition software that will take the spoken word of individuals and translate them into computer script has made life better for project managers. With this tool, they are able to fill out logs, create reports, and record all kinds of important project data.

Another aspect of voice recognition that enhances job-site productivity is the documentation necessary for a successful project. Project managers can apply this technology to record minutes, note attendance, and list actions taken. Then it becomes easy to distribute copies via the project intranet in a matter of minutes.

In addition, the system can be linked to your phone lines so that absent team members can contribute their views. As they also would be getting copies of the discussion, everyone involved is informed and can submit their input to the discussion.

Personal digital assistants (PDAs) and personal communication systems (PCSs)

New generations of PDAs and PCSs are doing remarkable things. They allow you to have a computer small enough to carry with you, relay information, document your activities during the day, and they are comfortable to use. The advantage of the PDA is that it uses wireless transmission to send and receive enormous amounts of project data to and from the job site. It can monitor material deliveries, check daily job scheduling and access reference material immediately. You can check your e-mail, send pager information, and keep on schedule.

Being more productive with limited resources can be accomplished easily and efficiently with a PDA. Safety reports, OSHA forms, and MSDS documents can be stored on them, and safety talks and videos can be viewed. Add to this the ability to maintain accurate records of inventory at all times and from all locations, organized by field, office, year, and supplier.

One of the most advantageous benefits of a PDA is the chance it gives you to communicate quickly with clients, the office, vendors, and employees. Integrate it with voice recognition technology, and you have a tool that can meet a variety of activities.

The same device can be your strategic planning tool to schedule appointments, maintain job leads and contacts, and document and track opportunities, allowing you to bring considerable organization to your frenetic life. Personal and professional areas of your life can be controlled and monitored with it. When you purchase a PDA, choose it by the applications you want to use daily, rather than the memory or hardware specifications.

PCSs traditionally have used cellular and digital wireless telephone technology and are quickly blending into PDAs. Growth in this market is being fueled by the rapid expansion of the telecommunications services that continue to push more services toward the PDAs. Two-way paging and the ability to send short alphanumeric messages are readily affordable. These devices are incorporating e-mail capability, voice mail, mailboxes, and fax capabilities.

Wireless technology has also changed mobile computing. Technology allows computer users to access anyone in the world from anywhere in the world without attaching to phone lines or other cables. New machines continue to get more powerful, thinner, and lighter. You can now use 3-D video, real-time conferencing, and DVD that will give you full motion video.

With corporations rapidly moving off the local area networks (LANs) and wide area networks (WANs) and onto the Internet, we will see LANs use the same protocols as the Internet (TCP/IP), turning companies into intranets. This will greatly assist the mobile worker today and tomorrow.

Many companies today produce personal digital assistants, or other electronic organizers. The provide an address book, an agenda, an expense tracker, a spreadsheet program, a sketch pad, and all sorts of time-saving devices. PDAs fit into a pocket, and utilize two small batteries.

Personal information managers

PIMs (personal information managers) have caught on with owners who want to have the ability to manage their jobs while utilizing "real-time conferencing" to allow several individuals involved with the project to access the same data and add input that is instantly available to the entire team. This technology has removed the traditional separation between design, construction, and the owner of the project. The designer, constructor, supplier, and owner can simultaneously review documents, solve problems, and work out the details being sketched out on the screen.

PIMs are capable of incorporating all segments of the job: inventory, daily logs, construction documents, planned versus as-built schedules, daily weather conditions, contractor-architect-engineer-supplier observations and information, current safety and building codes that are applicable to the job, daily/weekly status reports, job progress photos, shop drawing logs, complete specifications including substitutions, RFIs, payment status, change orders and extras, and communication documentation records.

Other powerful marketing software tools

There are also several software products that can change and simplify many of the most difficult tasks you have to do. But as software and hardware manufacturers are flooding the market with new programs and devices on almost a daily basis, were we to describe what is available today, it would change or perhaps vanish by the time you read this book. So, a general description of what you can find on the market is more appropriate:

- Decision-making software is available that can help you prioritize your leads and help you decide which goals and objects you need to concentrate on. Create a model of your situation by using one of the sample icons that represent variables in your decisions. Assign a numeric value to each. By following the directions, you will have a statistical analysis that will bring you to most the practical decision.

- Some devices give you the possibility of videoconferencing, just by attaching them to a notebook computer.

- Project management software will help you to track the project, delegate key business objects, strategies, and tactics, and monitor their status.

These new technologies have created a revolution in the business world. Gadgets are wonderful, but alone they are not enough. To enhance the benefits of these tools, you need to add your own talents—vision, flexibility, awareness, the realization of the value of relationships and, of course, as always, common sense.

Chapter

8

Marketing Communications Plan

This essential part of your marketing program cannot be overlooked. A *marketing communications plan* is a document that helps you to identify what it is about your company that will appeal to a prospective client. It enables you to get to know your target audience in great detail. It identifies which media outlets are best suited to reach your prospects and which best fit your budget. Then, it helps you find the best strategy for developing marketing materials that will drive your competitive advantages home in a way that will encourage prospective clients to take action.

The marketing communications plan will help you establish measurable goals. You will be able to define, in concrete dollars and cents terms, whether or not your marketing communications program is working.

Moreover, the marketing communications plan helps you establish consistency in all of your marketing materials. Once you develop a strategy of what messages you must communicate and to whom, you can make sure that all of your marketing materials have a consistency that will allow them to work in concert with one another to generate the results you want.

What is Marketing Communications?

Simply put, *marketing communications* consists of communication efforts designed to support marketing goals.

Marketing communications puts the two activities together. *Marketing communications materials* include anything you produce that communicates your marketing goals and objectives, such as your company brochures, newsletters, logos and stationery, direct mail, web site, and so on. Other marketing communications efforts, such as publicity, would be your attempt to use communications media, like newspapers, magazines, and newsletters, to accomplish your marketing goals.

Understanding the term marketing communications will also help you identify outside resources that will best serve your needs. There are several types of consultants involved with marketing, including sales trainers and marketing consultants. Likewise, there are several types involved with marketing communications. There are advertising agencies, whose primary function is to write, design, and place advertisements. There are public relations firms that produce and place stories in the media, and stage events for publicity. There are graphic designers, copywriters, web development firms, and specialists of all kinds. They are trained and experienced in the art of getting your message across to the outside world.

Companies that advertise themselves as marketing communications specialists typically provide a full range of services. They often integrate several marketing communications functions—advertising, publicity, and web development—to provide a complete package of marketing support.

Establishing Your Goals and Objectives

Before you decide whether or not you should print a brochure or build a web site, you must establish your goals and objectives. Goals, in this case, are marketing goals. You should have determined them when you developed your business and marketing plans. They define where you want to be in a given time period. Following are some examples of marketing goals:

- Enter a new geographic area and generate a backlog of $5 million in the coming 24 months.
- Introduce a new product or service to the marketplace in the coming year.
- Increase market share by five percent more than the past year.
- Generate a 50/50 mix of bid and negotiated work within the next two years.
- Become known as an expert in our field with the next 15 months.

From these goals you should establish clear-cut communication objectives.

Communications objectives are the responses you desire from your target audience. You should develop as many communications objectives as possible for each of your marketing goals. For instance, if entering a new geographic area and generating a backlog of $5 million within the next 24 months is your goal, the following communications objectives could be established for you:

- Create awareness of our company
- Create awareness of our product or services
- Establish the need for our product or services
- Communicate the benefits of our product or services
- Establish a liking or p reference for our product or services
- Generate inquiries

You will notice that each of these communications objectives works together to take the prospective buyer through the *decision-making process:* awareness, need, liking, purchase. It is essential that you take a prospect through each step of the process.

In addition to helping you decide what you must do to accomplish your goals, communications objectives help you *measure* your results. Determine how well you have accomplished each objective and decide whether the money you spent on marketing materials generated the results you expected. Your objectives will help you isolate which parts of your marketing communications plan are working and which are not.

Measuring results is not as easy as determining whether or not your *goals* have been met. If your goal was to enter a new market and generate $5 million in backlog within 24 months, and you failed to do so, it is not necessarily the fault of your marketing communications plan. Variables not controlled by the marketing communications plan—such as price, quality, your salespeoples' ability, and economic conditions—all may contribute to results. There may be market conditions, national crises, or international events that have affected everyone's business, which you could not possibly have factored into your plan.

What you *can* measure is whether you have met your communications objectives. Have you established awareness? Have you established liking or preference? Let's use the above example to illustrate how establishing objectives can allow you to measure your results.

To measure how well you create awareness of your company or your competitive advantages, you might conduct a random survey of prospective customers before the marketing communications campaign begins, and measure the percentage of your target audience that is aware of your company. After your campaign, you should conduct another random survey of a similar number of prospective customers to measure the percentage who are aware of your company and its services or products. Surveys, too, could measure whether your campaign has established *liking* or *preference* for your product or service. And, of course, if your objective is to generate responses, you can easily determine the number of responses in a given time period before and after your campaign.

Identifying Your Competitive Advantages

Every company that is at least modestly successful must have *competitive advantages:* characteristics of its products or services that make it better than or different from those of the competition. If you think you are just like another company, providing similar services, think again. You wouldn't be in business if there weren't something about your company that makes it different from the competition. Perhaps it is quality, or maybe price. Perhaps you have a technological edge, or perhaps you are well connected. Or it may be that the climate in your workplace is more pleasant than most and more conducive to your staff being challenged and providing more outreach to the clients. Your people, if they are happy in their jobs, work well as a team, and are helpful and pleasant to clients. This aura of goodwill has communicated itself to the public. This is an "edge" that most firms never consider—that the people your clients have contact with are the true ambassadors of goodwill!

Regardless, it is imperative that you *identify* your competitive advantages, because once you do, you will communicate them consistently in all your marketing efforts. Start by gathering a group of key people in your company, those who have either worked there a long while, interact often with clients, or have a good understanding of how you sell your products or services. Meet in a large conference room and set aside enough time to talk without interruption.

Get an easel with a pad of paper or use a marker board and create two columns. At the top of the left column, write "Competitive Advantages." Then brainstorm. Make a long list of all the characteristics that you feel are your company's strengths. They do not need to be unique to your company. They do not necessarily need to be tasks you do better than *every* other company, just areas in which you feel your company particularly excels. This list could be as long as you feel is necessary to identify all the characteristics, either individually or collectively, that set you apart.

Figure 8.1 shows a list of competitive advantages that a hypothetical interior construction company may identify.

1.   We have been in business over 30 years.

2.   Our people have significant experience in interior construction and renovation.

3.   We are innovators.

4.   We are good listeners.

5.   We have a flat organization chart.

6.   We have a lot of people with ownership in our company.

7.   We are extremely service oriented.

8.   We are committed to quality.

9.   We specialize in working in occupied spaces.

10. We are nice people to work with.

11. We are community divided.

Figure 8.1. Competitive advantages of a hypothetical interior construction company.

Once you have identified your competitive advantages, you must translate them into their *benefit* to your clients. This is essential. People buy the benefits they derive from a product or service, not the features of the product or service (see **Figure 8.2**). People don't use aspirin, for instance, because of its features: white, chalky, bitter tasting, dry, and round. People use aspirin because of the *benefit* they receive from using it—pain relief. Similarly, people don't buy an air conditioner because it is a large, clunky, metal box with fans, pipes, and coils. They buy cool air.

Your services are no different. Yet, all too often, companies, particularly in the A/E/C industry, promote the features of their products or services rather than the benefits derived from them. How often have you seen marketing materials that promote details like the experience of senior staff, experience building similar projects, pre-construction services, or quality craftsmanship? These may indeed be competitive advantages, but they are communicated in terms of *features* rather than benefits. However, people buy the *benefits* they will receive from these competitive advantages.

Here's a great way to hone you skills in focusing benefits over features. Remember that features describe a product or service, and benefits describe the reward people get from using your product or service.

After you have gathered your key staff and identified your company's competitive advantages, use this fun exercise to get used to focusing on benefits:

1. Give each person a new, nicely sharpened pencil.

2. Tell them you "discovered" this great new gadget and you think it has great sales potential – but you need their help. Act as if you have never seen this neat creation before and have some fun.

3. Make a chart with two columns. At the top left, write Features. On the top right, write Benefits.

4. Ask each person to study your neat new gizmo and describe a feature. You'll hear descriptions like, long, wooden, cylindrical, sharp and so on. If they say things like, "It erases," remind them that erases isn't a feature. Perhaps they meant, it has a rubber tip. Write the responses on the chart.

5. After you have generated a list of features, ask them to call out some benefits of the long, wooden stick. You'll probably hear things like "You can write with it." "It's easy to hold." "It erases mistakes." And so on. Write these responses on the chart, too.

6. Then ask the group, " what would be easier to sell?" A long, wooden, cylindrical sharp thing, or something that you can write with, that is easy to hold, and erases mistakes? Obviously, you could sell the latter easier.

While this may seem like a simplistic exercise, it is a memorable way of teaching the value of selling benefits over features. The same rules that apply to selling pencils apply to selling construction services.

Figure 8.2. Features versus benefits: wooden stick or writing tool.

The best way to identify the benefits of each of your competitive advantages is to submit it to the "So what?" test. For each advantage—experience, quality, and so forth—ask the question, "So what?" When the question is answered, again ask "So what?" and keep asking it. When you can no longer answer the "So what?" question, you have identified the real benefit. Here's how it works.

If your competitive advantage is "We have experience building similar projects," (a feature), ask, "So what?"

You might answer, "Well, that means we are familiar with what takes place during construction."

"So what?"

"It means we have faced similar challenges and know how to solve them."

"So what?"

"Well, we should have less down time and fewer change orders."

"So what?"

"We'll deliver the project faster at a better price."

"So what?"

"The client will save money and generate income on their completed project sooner."

That's the real benefit. Your experience on similar projects (a feature) allows your client to save money and generate income sooner, which is a benefit (see **Figure 8.3**).

These two words – So what – will forever help you be a better seller. Whether or not you ever write a word of ad copy or text on a Web page, understanding how to identify the benefits of the products or services you sell will enable you to prepare better presentations, get to the sale quicker, and understand your prospects' needs faster.

Anytime you need to convert competitive advantages that are stated as features into benefits, apply the So what? Test. If your competitive advantage is quality, ask, "So what?"

You may answer, "Well, if we concentrate on quality, the owner gets a better building."

Ask again, "So what?"

You will ponder the questions, perhaps get a little annoyed, and then answer, "Well, a better building requires less maintenance."

"So what?" you demand of yourself.

Now, starting to see the light, you answer, "Well, less maintenance means less expense for the owner."

"So what?"

"Less expense means more money."

"So what?" You ask again.

But this time, there is no answer. Congratulations, you have arrived at the real benefit. You help your clients make more money by delivering better-quality building that require less maintenance. Now that is a competitive advantage an owner can warm up to.

Print the words So what? Large and in bold type on a sheet of paper and tape it to the wall of your office. It will always remind you to zero in on benefits, whenever you sell.

Figure 8.3. The "So what?" exercise.

You may think people would be able to determine the benefits for themselves. But in reality, people are too busy to analyze situations. What seems important to you may not be important to them. You therefore have to tell them why your competitive advantage will make their lives better.

Most purchases, food, clothing, a car, or concrete pavement, are responses to the benefits people receive from the product or service offered. If you can show how your product or service can satisfy a prospect's needs, you will be far closer to the sale.

Now, apply the "So what?" test to each of the competitive advantages you wrote on your chart. Your competitive advantages were listed on the left side. Under "Competitive Advantages," write "Features," with a red marker. This will remind you that your competitive advantages are *features*, not the characteristics you should be using to sell your products or services.

At the top of the right column, write "Benefits." For each feature you listed, apply the "So what?" test. Keep asking, "So what?" until you have exhausted all your answers. At the end, you should have identified the one benefit that prospective customers can relate to. You may find that the same benefit applies to many of the competitive advantages you have listed.

As you proceed, you will find a cultural change taking place among the people involved in the brainstorming exercise. They will begin thinking in terms of benefits instead of features, and finding ways to communicate the benefit of what they do for the company's clients. As they go out and promote your company, either as marketers, salespeople, or project managers, they will begin communicating this message on a daily basis to clients, who will then be better able to relate to the services your company provides.

Figure 8.4 shows how the "So what?" test would reveal the benefits of the competitive advantages listed for the hypothetical interior contractor in **Figure 8.1**.

Competitive advantages	Benefits
1. We have been in business for over 30 years.	1. We've conquered almost every construction challenge, which saves our clients time and money.
2. Our people have significant experience in interior construction and renovation.	2. We won't make "rookie" mistakes, which delivers our jobs faster and helps our clients get money sooner.
3. We are innovators.	3. We find ways to improve the construction process, which saves time and money for our clients.
4. We are good listeners.	4. We won't make careless mistakes, which brings the project in on time and within budget.
5. We have a flat organizational chart.	5. Our clients work with decision makers, which minimizes mistakes and expedites jobs, saving them time and money.
6. We have a lot of people with ownership in the company.	6. Our people have a more personal stake in the success of our projects, which increases client service and improves quality.
7. We are extremely service oriented.	7. We always let clients know what is going on with their project, minimizing stress.
8. We are committed to quality.	8. A quality project requires fewer change orders and repairs, improving the investment value of our clients' properties.
9. We specialize in working in occupied spaces.	9. We know the challenges, keep work areas clean, and minimize errors, thus maximizing the chance of on-time, within budget delivery.
10. We nice people to work with.	10. We make a usually stressful experience more pleasant for our clients.
11. We are community minded.	11. By helping people and businesses locally, we are helping the local economy and creating business opportunities for our clients. Also, by caring for others, they see we care for them as well.

Figure 8.4. Competitive advantages and benefits of a hypothetical interior construction company.

You will probably become aware of a distinct trend emerging when you begin identifying benefits. The first is that there are relatively few benefits to which people react. The second is that you need to describe how the client receives the benefit.

The key selling point

After you have identified the benefits of all of your competitive advantages, you must now identify the *key selling point,* the one that is more important than any others.

Although you may feel that many of your competitive advantages are key, it is important to identify the one that is most important, because when you or your consultants are creating advertisements, direct mailers, brochures, and so on, you need to be able to prioritize your advantages. An effective advertisement, for instance, must communicate one selling point clearly and then provide additional supportive selling points if needed.

If you do nothing else when preparing marketing materials, you must be sure to communicate your key selling point. By identifying it early on, you will always know which competitive advantage *must* be communicated in all your marketing materials.

After you have identified the key selling point, identify a few other selling points that you feel will need to be included in your marketing communications efforts. These will probably be the three or four most important *additional* benefits that you identified earlier.

Always write out your selling points in sentence form. This not only allows you to write complete thoughts, it will form the basis of your body copy for advertisements and other marketing communications materials well in advance. With this kind of preparation, you will always be ready with a promotion when you need one.

Defining Your Target Audience

Once you have established your goals and objectives, and identified the benefits of your competitive advantages, you need to determine your *target audience,* the group of people most likely to buy your products or services. Note the words, "people *most likely* to buy." Your target audience is not *every* potential buyer but rather, those who would benefit *most* from your particular products or services and who would respond best to your competitive advantages.

Recognizing that you probably have more than one target audience, it is a good idea to prioritize the groups in terms of primary target audience, secondary target audience, and so on. This will help you allocate your resources, concentrating most of your time and money on researching the primary target audience.

Demographics and psychographics

A target audience is defined by its demographic and psychographic characteristics.

Demographic characteristics are those that can be measured or quantified. They include characteristics like business type, geographic location, number of employees, annual revenue, and even specific job titles within the organization. Demographic characteristics are relatively easy to identify.

Psychographic characteristics group people into homogenous segments based on their psychological makeup and lifestyle characteristics. They might include such factors as interests, hobbies, beliefs, and so on. Psychographic characteristics, although they are more difficult to define, are often more important than demographic characteristics. Purchase decisions, even those made by businesspeople, are based on how a product can satisfy the buyer's needs. Understanding prospective buyers' psychographic traits will help you understand their needs and how your product or service can satisfy those needs.

When first defining your target audience, start with broad definitions. If you are an interior contractor, perhaps your primary target audience will be space users. Your secondary target audience may be interior architects because they often have some influence in the selection of an interior contractor. Further, you may feel commercial brokers, property managers, developers, and even base-building general contractors might comprise your tertiary target market.

Once you have decided what type of people fall within your target markets, you should further narrow your definition to best suit your particular competitive advantages. Start with their *demographic characteristics*.

In the case of the interior contractor mentioned above, perhaps you are best at building office interiors that are between 1,000 and 20,000 square feet. Furthermore, you may have determined that you want to pursue negotiated projects because you don't have the resources to prepare quantities of lump-sum bids, and you have narrowed your geographic scope to a 50-mile radius of your office to provide the best level of service.

Based on these specifics, you can narrow the demographic characteristics of your target audience. If you build office spaces between 1,000 and 20,000 square feet, you can determine the size of the companies you wish to target. You might do this by phoning a friend who is a broker and asking how many square feet of office space a typical employee occupies. The answer might be that typically, each employee uses about 200 square feet, when factoring in common areas. Doing a little math, you would then know that your target audience consists of companies having between 5 and 100 employees.

Further narrowing your target, you might assume that a facility or office manager in each of these companies would make decisions about hiring an interior contractor. Realizing that there are more office managers than facility managers at the smaller firms, you might decide to target them. You reason that even if there is not an office manager at some companies, inquiries sent to office managers will be forwarded to someone with those responsibilities.

Because you have decided to pursue negotiated work, you can eliminate certain types of businesses, such as government agencies. By narrowing your geographic range to a 50-mile radius, you can identify specific counties or towns to target.

You should also narrow your secondary and tertiary target audiences in the same manner. If your secondary target audience consists of interior architects, you might assume that an interior architecture company of any size would have clients in the range of the office space users you are pursuing, so you would not qualify those companies by their size.

You realize, however, that there is more than one decision-maker in each firm, so you decide to include all the architects in each firm. If, when quantifying your target audience, you determine that the total number of interior architects is too large to reasonably pursue, you can narrow your audience to senior architects.

In summary, for the above example, the demographic profile of your target audience might be as follows:

Primary target audience

- Office space users
- Private-sector companies with between five and 100 employees
- People with the title of office manager
- Companies in the nearest three counties

Secondary target audience

- Interior architecture firms
- All interior architects within those firms
- Companies in the three nearest counties

Tertiary target audiences

- Commercial brokerage companies
- All brokers in those companies
- Commercial real estate developers
- Project management positions in those companies
- Base building general contractors
- Estimators in those companies
- Project managers in those companies

Narrowing your target audience in this way is important for at least two reasons. First, it keeps you from wasting your time chasing prospective clients who may not be a good match for your services. Second, when it comes time to develop or purchase a mailing list of prospects, you have quantifiable parameters that a mail list seller can use to build a list for you.

Once you have a clear understanding of your target audience in demographic terms, you should attempt to determine their *psychographic characteristics*. Psychographics are not as important in business-to-business selling as they are in consumer selling. Often, when buying consumer products, people make purchasing decisions based on how a product satisfies some emotional need. In business, people buy the benefits derived from a product. Sometimes those benefits are emotional, like stress reduction. But more often than not, the benefits are business details, like saving time or money.

In this manner, it is possible to develop a loose description of the psychographic characteristics of your target audience based upon your competitive advantages. If you feel that your honest dealings with clients and high level of customer service are your strengths, your target audience's psychographic characteristics might include an appreciation for being taken care of by someone who is straightforward. Although you will not find such details when purchasing mailing lists, if in your own research you can learn any pertinent details about your target audience, it would pay you well to do so. Knowing your target audience's psychographic characteristics will help you find the best language with which to communicate to them.

Speaking to one person

After describing your target audience's demographic and psychographic characteristics in some detail, you must try to narrow your definition to *one person*. This is an exercise that will prove tremendously valuable when you begin developing your marketing materials.

Why identify one person when even your carefully defined target audience still contains a diverse mix of people? Imagining one person helps you learn how to communicate more effectively with him or her.

Which is a more effective way of communicating: speaking to a group of 1,000 people, or speaking with one person? When you speak to one person, you can establish eye contact and get to know that person's likes and dislikes. You can get feedback on what you are saying about your company, and you can establish a relationship. In this way, you can customize your presentation to suit individual needs.

When you speak to a crowd, you cannot make this type of connection. You can only make general assumptions about their needs. And, unless they are throwing tomatoes at you, you rarely get a sense of whether or not you are saying things that will have much impact.

If you think of your target audience in the same way, when you create your marketing materials—your advertisements, brochures, newsletters, or web site—you must write as if you are speaking to a single person. You aren't talking to the masses but rather to one individual who can react to your message. This is the principal device used by the greatest of "master" speakers, who had compelling messages to convey and who conveyed them magnificently. (Read some of the books written about great speakers, such as Franklin Delano Roosevelt and Winston Churchill. They had one of the most dramatic messages of all time to convey: supporting a war!)

Try the exercise of identifying your target audience as one person. Are you speaking to a man or a woman? How old is he? Is she single or married? What is her job title? Is he an "influencer," someone who likes to be the first to buy things, then tell friends and colleagues about his purchase experience? How long has he held his position? What are her hobbies? Does he play golf or tennis? How tall is she?

By doing this, you will begin to see one person in your mind, and your communication efforts will become more personal and subsequently more effective. Thus, there will be something in your message, whether written or spoken, that will appeal to every person who reads or hears it.

Developing a Creative Strategy Statement

By now, you should have established your communication objectives, determined your competitive advantages and stated them in terms of their benefits, identified your key selling point, and defined your target audience by its demographic and psychographic characteristics. In other words, you should have a fairly good sense of what you want to accomplish, what you want to say about your company, and to whom you want to speak.

Now it is time to decide *how* you want to say it. Before you create your marketing materials, you need to develop a sense of the look and feel of the materials so they can best convey your competitive advantages and speak to your target audience.

The best way to do this is to develop a *creative strategy statement*. This statement simply explains what you want to accomplish, what you want to say, to whom you want to say it, and how you should communicate it. How you communicate will take some thought. The creative strategy statement does not ask you to decide what specifically to say and how to design materials.

It simply asks you to determine the overall look and feel of your effort. For the interior contractor example mentioned in this chapter, a creative strategy statement may sound something like this:

> *Our objective is to establish preference for our services and generate sales opportunities by communicating that our company is the best interior design contractor for privately held companies with five to 100 employees, particularly if they need work done in occupied spaces. We will speak primarily to people within these companies who have little experience in retrofitting their office spaces. Because they are probably anxious about this process, we will create marketing materials that communicate how choosing us will ease their minds. We will try to use visual images and text that show how we will make their lives easier if they choose us.*

You can see from the above example that while specific visual images and text have not been decided, the people who create the marketing materials will have a very good sense of what you want to accomplish. In fact, ideas for visuals and copy may pop into your mind as you read it.

Writing your creative strategy statement may be a challenging task, and it may take several revisions. However, once you do it, you will have a clear idea of how you will conduct your entire marketing communications campaign.

Producing a Creative Platform

Now, it is time to put all the information you have gathered into a format that can be used by your team and the contractors who are helping you in developing marketing communications materials. You will now create a document called a *creative platform*. The creative platform is essentially an outline that lists your (1) marketing goals and the communication objectives that will achieve them; (2) competitive advantages, stated in terms of their benefits; (3) key selling point; (4) other selling points; (5) target audience, defined in demographic and psychographic terms; and (6) creative strategy statement. **Figure 8.5** is an example of a creative platform.

The creative platform is a guide that takes you from where you are to where you want to be. It is the guide that tells the sailor how to let the wind catch the sails to get from the dock to an island hideaway. It will give your creative team the information it needs to prepare marketing communications materials that convey the right message, delivered to the right audience.

The platform is especially helpful if more than one person or consultant is working on your marketing materials. It allows the group to work from the same strategy and create materials that will work together to accomplish the desired results. For example, if you decide to create a new logo, an advertisement, a web site, and a publicity campaign, you may use different people to perform each of these functions because they utilize different skills. The creative platform will ensure that all of these marketing efforts will have the same look and feel and convey the same important points.

Marketing Goals
To generate a backlog of $5 million within the next 24 months

Communications Objectives
- Create awareness of our economy ?
- Create awareness of out interior contracting services
- Establish the need for our services
- Communicate the benefits of our services
- Establish a preference for our services
- Generate inquiries

Competitive Analysis
1. We've conquered almost every construction challenge, which saves our clients time and money.
2. We won't make mistakes from lack of experience, which saves our clients time and money.
3. We find ways to improve the construction process, which saves our clients time and money.
4. We won't make careless mistakes, which ensures the project will be completed on time and within budget.
5. Our clients work with decision makers, which minimizes mistakes and expedites jobs, saving them time and money.
6. People have a more personal stake in the success of our company, ensuring that they will focus on client satisfaction.
7. We always let clients know what is going on with their project, minimizing their stress.
8. A quality project requires fewer change orders and repairs, improving the investment value of our clients' properties.
9. We know the challenges of working in occupied spaces, keep work areas tidy and dust free, and minimize the risk of error, thus maximizing the prospect of on-time, within budget delivery.
10. We make a usually stressful experience more pleasant for our clients.
11. By helping people and businesses locally, we are helping the local economy and creating business opportunities for our clients.

Key Selling Point
We know the challenges of working in occupied spaces, keep work areas tidy and dust free, and minimize the risk of error, thus maximizing the prospect of on-time, within budget delivery.

Other Selling Points
- We have a flat organizational chart. Our clients work with decision makers, which minimizes mistakes and expedites the job, saving them time and money.
- We build quality. A quality project requires fewer change orders and repairs, improving the investment value of our clients' properties.
- We have experience. We've conquered almost every construction challenge, which saves our clients time and money.

Target Audience
Primary target audience
- Office space users
- Private-sector companies of between 5 and 100 employees
- People with the title of office manager
- Companies in Sonoma, La Jolla and Bristol counties.

Secondary target audience
- Interior architecture firms
- All interior architects within those firms
- Companies in Sonoma, La Jolla and Bristol counties.

Figure 8.5. Creative platform of a hypothetical interior construction company.

Tertiary target audience
- Commercial brokerage companies
- All brokers within those companies
- Commercial real estate developers
- Project management positions within those companies
- Base building general contractors
- Estimators within those companies
- Project managers within those companies

Creative Strategy Statement

To establish preference for our services and generate sales opportunities by communicating that we are the best interior contractor for private companies with 5 to 100 employees, particularly if they need work done in occupied spaces. We will speak primarily to people within these companies who have little experience in retrofitting their office space. Because they are probably very anxious about this process, we will create marketing materials that communicate how choosing us will ease their minds. We will try to use visual images and text that show how we will make their life easier if they choose us.

Figure 8.5. Creative platform of a hypothetical interior construction company, (continued).

The creative platform and the project manager of a construction company have similar functions: defining a project's goals and objectives and combining a diverse group of skilled craftspeople to achieve these goals.

Give a copy of your creative platform to each of the people who are to develop your marketing materials, and you will see that each of the elements work together. If you do not want to prepare the creative platform or any of its elements yourself, make sure that your in-house creative staff or outside consultants do it for you *before* they prepare any of your marketing communications materials. Have them show it to you, of course, before any action is taken. Use it as a guide. If, at any time, there are questions about which direction to take, refer to the creative platform. Use it as a guide to ensure that your marketing materials are consistent and stay on track.

Ensuring Ease, Efficiency, and Effectiveness

Taking the time to determine your communication objectives, define your competitive advantages, isolate a key selling point, identify your target audience, prepare a creative strategy statement, and produce a creative platform will save you untold time and marketing dollars as you prepare your marketing communications materials. It will also ensure that everything you prepare will be as effective as it possibly can be.

Congratulations. You have graduated with honors from Marketing Communications 101. From here, you can move with confidence into developing your marketing communications materials and other marketing communications efforts.

Chapter

9

Marketing Materials

All too often, people decide they want to produce advertisements, a brochure, or a web site before they determine their objectives and identify their target audience. Yet, your objectives and your target audience play key roles in determining which promotional materials will be most effective. It is imperative that you go through the process of developing a marketing communications plan first.

This chapter discusses a wide variety of promotional materials and gives you guidance about which will be the most effective and cost efficient for meeting your goals and objectives. After describing each, you will learn the steps involved in producing marketing communications materials, and will read recommendations about what you can do yourself and what you may need help with, either from your existing staff or outside contractors.

Advertisements, for instance, are effective for accomplishing the objective of establishing awareness but are not effective for generating action. A brochure is good for creating desire and action, but it is wasted if your objective is creating awareness. Web sites, too, are good for creating desire and interest but not effective for creating awareness.

The size and geographic diversity of your target audience also affect which marketing materials to develop. For example, publicity is effective for reaching a broad target audience, whereas direct mail is best when you have a small and clearly defined target audience. These are but a few of the considerations you will need to make before deciding which marketing communications or promotional materials to create for your marketing program.

The Role of Marketing Materials in the Decision-Making Process

To sell a product or service, you must take a prospective buyer through the decision-making process. There are four steps to the process, and a prospect must go through each step every time he or she buys:

1. awareness,
2. interest,
3. desire, and
4. action.

When you develop a strategy for achieving your communications objectives, you should make sure that the marketing communications materials you select take prospects completely through the process. You may feel, for instance, that you have already achieved awareness in the geographic area that you are targeting. Your strategy, then, would focus on developing materials that take prospects through the entire decision-making process. **Table 9.1** shows how different marketing communications materials are used to help people through the decision-making process.

Kinds of Marketing Communications Materials

There are dozens of different kinds of marketing communications materials you can use to accomplish your objectives. Generally, the ones used most often in the A/E/C industry are (1) advertising, (2) collateral material, (3) direct mail, (4) publicity, (5) Internet, (6) exhibits, and (7) presentations.

Each of these satisfies different objectives and helps you reach different target audiences. What becomes clear after learning about each of their strengths and weaknesses is that in most cases you will have to execute a strategy that includes more than one type of marketing communications material to accomplish your objectives. **Table 9.2** will give you a quick understanding of the advantages and disadvantages of some of the primary forms of marketing communications.

	Awareness	Interest	Desire	Action
Advertising				
Magazines and newspapers	X	X		
Directories (e.g., Yellow Pages)			X	X
Radio and TV	X	X		
Outdoor (Billboard)	X			
Collateral Material				
Brochures		X	X	
Video and audio tapes		X	X	
CD-ROMs		X	X	
Software		X	X	
Article reprints		X	X	
Signs	X			
Bumper stickers and decals	X			
Direct Mail				
Stand alone	X	X	X	X
Group (e.g., deck cards)	X	X		
Exhibits				
Trade shows		X	X	X
Public shows		X	X	
Internet				
Web sites		X	X	X
Web directories		X	X	
Web advertising	X	X		
Premiums (virtually all types)	X			
Presentations				
Personal selling			X	X
Speeches (public meetings)	X	X	X	
Seminars and conferences	X	X	X	
Public relations				
News releases	X	X		
Industry representatives role	X	X		
Telemarketing (out- and inbound)		X	X	X

Reprinted with permission of The Aberdeen Group

Table 9.1. Fitting promotional tools into the purchase process.

	Advantages	Disadvantages
Advertising	Reaches a broad audience	Cannot target small groups
	Low cost-per-thousand (CPM) impressions	Can be expensive overall
	You control the message	
Collateral materials	Reaches targeted audience	Not good for introducing company
	Excellent way to showcase you work	High CPM
	You control the message	Limited credibility
Public relations	Reaches a broad audience	Cannot target small groups
	Low or no CPM	Risk of no return on investment
	Maximum credibility	Cannot control what gets published
Direct mail	Reaches a targeted audience	Can miss some prospects
	Little risk of wasted investment	High CPM Limited credibility
	You control the message	
Internet	Reaches a broad audience	Cannot target small groups
	Low CPM	Can be expensive overall
	You control the message	Limited credibility
Exhibit	Reaches a targeted audience	Can miss some prospects
	Little risk of wasted investment	High CPM
	You control the message	Limited credibility

Table 9.2. Advantages and disadvantages of various marketing communications materials.

Advertising

Advertising is one of the most common forms of promotion. It can take many shapes. The most commonly used are print advertising in magazines and newspapers; directory advertising, which includes Yellow Pages advertising; broadcast advertising on radio or television; and outdoor advertising, typically on billboards.

Although advertising is quite common in consumer sales and some business sales, contractors and subcontractors do not often use it. Perhaps this is because it is hard to measure whether or not advertising can be credited for generating big-ticket purchases such as concrete formwork or an office building. Nevertheless, advertising has long proven its effectiveness for establishing awareness, interest, and desire and should be factored into most companies' marketing communications efforts.

Advertising is a *broadcast* medium. It reaches a broad audience. You cannot specify who will see or hear your advertisement. You can narrow the audience that will be exposed to it by selecting *media* that are targeted to a specific audience, such as neighborhood newspapers, trade association magazines, or news-format radio stations, but you cannot preselect who, in this large audience, will see or hear your advertisement. This can be advantageous if you are trying to reach a broad audience and want to establish awareness and name recognition fairly quickly. Name recognition, you will find, can be an important factor. However, this type of advertising is less advantageous if the audience you want to reach is small and focused. If you're targeting an audience that runs in the millions, this is an excellent medium. If you are aiming at a few thousand (or hundreds of) specific people, you're using an elephant gun to catch a rabbit.

When producing advertisements, you can control the message you present to your target audience. Because you write and design it, you will be certain of the message it presents to your target audience. This is obviously important when you have a specific message you are trying to send.

Advertising messages are always fleeting; in other words, as soon as they are seen or heard, they are gone. This is particularly a problem with electronic media such as television or radio. The listener cannot mull over the message or review it to clarify facts. (This is one of the reasons advertising on television is so expensive. For a message to be effective, it must be repeated over and over again, sometimes several times in the same program.) Print advertising allows the prospect to re-read a message. Publications with longer "shelf lives," like magazines and directories, afford even better opportunities for people to see your advertisement more than once.

However, because people who see or hear your advertisement know that you wrote it (or someone wrote it for you), advertising generally has limited credibility. You can enhance the credibility of your advertisements by including third-party testimonials. People believe what others say about you more than what you say about yourself. That is why so many commercials for consumer products show endorsements of people who use the product.

Another advantage of advertising is its low cost-per-thousand impressions. No other marketing communications vehicle is less expensive per person reached than advertising, with the possible exception of media publicity. This can be a great advantage if you are trying to target a large audience that can be reached via one newspaper or magazine. However, the overall cost of placing advertisements can sometimes be too expensive for some companies. Even though a publication may reach a large number of prospects, firm owners often think that the overall cost is too high, so they choose a more direct, less expensive approach.

According to industry professional and author Daniel P. Anderson, magazine advertising is good for creating awareness and interest. Most PR people agree that placing ads in magazines may generate name recognition but they do not expect to make sales from this kind of promotion. (Those who do professional advertising call these "institutional ads" and know that their sole purpose is to make the company visible.) The possible exception to this concept is directory advertising, such as the Yellow Pages, because prospects are predisposed to buy when they use such directories. They have already established interest in a product, and they will review directory ads to identify who supplies the products or services they are looking for, and will learn about the competitive advantages of various vendors through their advertising messages.

Typically, however, advertising supports other marketing materials. It is used to create awareness and reach a broad group of people within a target audience. Other forms of promotion should then be used to create desire and generate action.

Selecting the right advertising medium

Deciding where to place your advertisements takes a combination of common sense, creativity, and research. Once you have defined your target audience, think about the media that might influence them. Ask yourself:

- ♦ Which magazines and newspapers do my prospects read?

- ♦ Are there any general-interest business publications in my city or region?

- ♦ Are there newspapers that focus solely on real estate?

- ♦ What trade or professional associations have members in our target audience?

- ♦ Do they have publications that accept advertising?

- ♦ Are there industry directories that prospects use to buy our products or services?

Once you have identified some of the more obvious advertising vehicles, try to think of some of the less obvious ones:

♦ Are there any cable television shows that our target audience might be likely to watch?

♦ Are there any radio stations that reach our target audience or any segments of radio programs targeted to them?

♦ Are there any regional issues or sections of large newspapers, like the daily newspaper, that offer discounts if ads are placed there exclusively? For instance, it costs less to place a regional advertisement in *The Wall Street Journal* than in some local business newspapers.

♦ Are there any private schools that produce publications that may be read by people in our target audience?

♦ Are billboards a viable option?

♦ Is mass transit something to consider, particularly in routes heavily populated by our target audience?

You also can conduct research that will help you identify media sources. Most libraries carry the *Standard Rate and Data Service* (SRDS), a multi-volume directory (also accessible via the web at **www.srds.com.**). SRDS is considered the ultimate resource for advertising media buyers. This directory is divided into business and consumer publications and is organized by topic. Each listing offers a brief profile, editor's name, and complete contact information, and it lists media by subject and location. If you want to find publications that focus on facility management, for instance, you can find a comprehensive list there.

Inside the guide you will discover the mission of the publication, advertising costs and deadlines, editorial calendars when available, and contact information. You can phone their representatives to get more detailed information about the readers to determine if they fall within the definition of your target audience. Additionally, SRDS contains advertising rate information for newspapers, magazines, television, radio, and other media.

Identifying the right medium in which to advertise is half the battle. The other half is determining how often you should run your ads, and also determining the cost of purchasing the ad space or time, depending on whether you are using print or broadcast media.

Complicated media buys—ones that involve multiple geographic markets and a wide mix of print and broadcast—might best be left to experienced advertising agencies or media buying consultants. Ad agencies have the expertise to both create the ads and identify and purchase the ad space. Typically, they will charge for their creative services and purchase the ad space for you.

Most publications or radio or TV stations remit a 15 percent commission to ad agencies, which the agencies use to pay for their time in identifying media, creating a media plan, and buying the media space for each advertisement.

However, most often, people in the A/E/C business make fairly simple media buys and can pay for the cost of the advertisement directly. Often, the vendor you've selected will give you the agency commission. In fact, you should insist upon it if you are doing their work for them.

Frequency discounts are given when an advertiser commits to multiple ad purchases within a contract period, usually a year. Purchasing a single ad will cost you more than purchasing three or more, which is more expensive than purchasing six, and so on. (Note that anyone who has been advertising for years will tell you that a single advertisement anywhere is pointless. It is only repetition that will establish your name and reputation.) If you plan to run more than one ad, take advantage of frequency discounts by signing an *advertising contract* for multiple insertions. If you cannot honor the stipulations in the contract by inserting multiple ads, you will be held responsible for paying only the difference between the ad rate you contracted for and what you would have paid for fewer insertions. This is called a *short rate* and usually does not carry a penalty.

You can often negotiate with your vendor to get a lower rate than they normally offer. Unsold ad space is like an unsold hotel room or airline seat. Once the publication is printed, unsold ad revenue is lost. So often, the vendor will negotiate by selling you an ad at a lower frequency rate than you will actually use.

If you decide to do your own purchasing of advertising space, talk to the *sales representatives* at the print or broadcast medium in which you are interested. These people are generally friendly, knowledgeable, and cooperative, and are almost always willing to work with you to figure the best specific issues to advertise in, for print media, and to help you get the best rates. Don't forget. They'd like you to come back!

Just make sure to gather information on all potential media in which you may likely advertise. Make your selection based on which has the readers, listeners, or viewers that best match your target audience, the most credibility, and which offers the lowest cost per thousand. Try not to be persuaded to select one medium over another simply because of a good sales pitch from a representative. We all know of salespeople who oversell a product or service.

Print advertising

Like any creative skill, writing and designing effective advertisements takes a great deal of training and experience. You would probably be best served to find a good, creative ad agency or marketing communications firm that understands your business and the needs of your clients and then negotiate a fair price to produce your advertisements or campaign. However, if your budget does not allow it, or if you simply want to be able to judge whether the advertisements produced by your consultant are effective, you should understand the basics of creating advertising.

First and foremost, effective advertisements must meet your communications objectives to generate the desired results. They don't necessarily need to win awards for creativity. After you have created your advertisement, ask yourself if it will satisfy your communications objectives. If not, refine it until it does.

Writing the ad

There are three principal parts of any effective advertisement: the *headline,* the *visual,* and the *body copy.* They must work in concert to communicate your key selling point, which is the most important one of your competitive advantages.

In most ad agencies, a designer, being more visually oriented, will work with a copywriter to develop ideas for headlines and visuals. The visual and the headline must work synergistically to clearly convey your competitive advantage. If you are creating the ad yourself, make a simple list with two columns, one for the visual and the other for the headline. If you are more visual than verbal, start with ideas for photos or illustrations and then try to develop a headline that works with them. If you are better with words, start with a headline. You should come up with a few options from which to choose.

Figure 9.1 shows a list of ideas for visuals and headlines for the hypothetical interior contractor we have invented. The contractor's *key selling point* is: *We know the challenges of working in occupied spaces, keep work areas tidy and dust-free, and minimize the risk of error, thus maximizing the prospect of on-time, within-budget delivery.*

Key Selling Point

We know the challenges of working in occupied spaces, keep work areas tidy and dust-free, and minimize the risk of error, thus maximizing the prospect of on-time, within-budget delivery.

Other Selling Points

- We have a flat organization chart. Our clients work with decision makers, which minimizes mistakes and expedites the job, saving time and money.

- We build quality. A quality project requires fewer change orders and repairs, improving the investment value of our clients' properties.

- We have experience. We've conquered almost every construction challenge, which saves our clients time and money.

Visuals	Headlines
1. A construction worker wearing a hardhat and dressed in a maid's apron, dusting a desk.	1. We'll keep your office so clean you'll think we're really maids
2. A pristine office with yellow construction tape all around.	2. Just because you need to renovate your office doesn't mean it has to be a mess.
3. A busy office environment with construction workers all around.	3. We have so much experience building in occupied spaces, you'll hardly notice we're around.

Figure 9.1. Visual and headline ideas for a hypothetical interior contractor, Certified Construction, Inc.

The best *headlines* are those that grab attention. The same is true of visuals as well. But if an ad headline only grabs attention, it is only doing half its job. A headline must also convey your key selling point.

People usually scan advertisements. Unless your headline gives them a compelling reason to read your ad by telling them something that relates to their needs, they'll turn the page. If your headline is provocative, but doesn't say anything about your selling point, chances are that people won't read further.

If your headline grabs attention because it is either clever or written powerfully and is able to convey your key selling point, you have already won more than half the battle. If all the reader does is read your headline, understand your selling point, and see your company's name on the ad, you will have succeeded. If readers study the visual and read the body copy, you've hit a home run.

There are many different kinds of headlines. Some of the more common are:

1. *Factual.* The headline powerfully states your selling point. *Certified Construction has experience renovating occupied office space.* It may not be clever, but it is clear.

2. *Analogy.* The headline takes your selling point and uses an analogy that makes for an intriguing statement. *We'll keep your office so clean you'll think we're really maids.*

3. *Testimonials.* Because people are more inclined to believe things that others say about you more than what you say about yourself, headlines that use testimonials are very effective. *"Certified kept our office so clean during renovation, we hardly knew they were there."— Deborah Carper, American Marketing Association.*

4. *Play on words.* These types of headlines take an aspect of your selling point and throw in a double meaning or pun to capture attention. *Certified finished our workspace while we finished our work.*

Many people see the *visual* part of an ad before they read the copy, so an attention-getting visual is crucial to the effectiveness of your ad.

Visuals are attention-getting when they have a twist of some kind that makes them unexpected. If you don't want to use a visual with a twist, you should at least have a visual that is bold and graphic. A powerful photograph, a collage, or an illustration can be visceral and extremely effective.

Consider the publication(s) in which the ad will appear. You don't want your ad to look like every other one. If you are placing an ad in a real estate publication, avoid a straightforward photo of an office building, for instance. There will probably be 25 other such photos, thus yours will not stand out.

No matter what kind of visual you use, it must communicate your key selling point. A common mistake people make is to show a picture of completed work in their ad rather than illustrate their key selling point. For instance, if their selling point is how well they work in occupied office space, rather than use a visual that supports it, they simply show a picture of a pretty, completed office interior. It may be attractive but it doesn't convey your selling point, thus your ad may be a total a waste of money. Instead, use a photo of your people at work renovating the space while the employees of the firm are doing their jobs *undisturbed!*

Coming up with an idea for an attention-getting visual takes time. It is, however, time well spent. Creative advertising is not a gift that every individual possesses. It may take hours or days of staring into space, doodling and twisting ideas and words around before you "get" the perfect concept. A good visual is probably the most important part of your advertisement and without that "lightbulb" idea, don't waste your time or money.

The *body copy* of an advertisement—the words that follow the headline—is generally divided into four parts: the *lead, body, wrap,* and *call to action.*

The *lead* is the first sentence or two. The lead acts as a transition from the headline to the body of the ad by explaining the headline. A lead sentence for the first headline in **Figure 9.1,** "We'll keep your office so clean you'll think we're really maids," might be *"Despite what you may have heard, at Certified, we are really builders. It's just that we keep the offices we renovate so clean that our customers sometimes think we are maids."* See how the lead sentences explain the headline?

Following the lead sentences is the *body* of the ad. It serves to explain your other selling points to the reader. It can be as simple as a few sentences, each dedicated to describing one of your competitive advantages in descending order of importance. If you wrote your other selling points in sentence form, you can practically plug them in here. Body copy for the lead sentences above might be:

♦ *"In addition to a clean office space, we build a top-quality office. Quality construction means fewer repairs, which improves the value of your office investment."*

♦ *"With more than 30 years of experience, we've conquered almost every construction challenge, which saves our clients time and money. And when you work with us, you will work with top decision-makers in our company, which minimizes mistakes and expedites the job, saving you time and money."*

You can see how this body copy is only slightly modified from the way the interior contractor's other selling points were written. They flow nicely and let you get a few more competitive advantages across to the reader without being boring.

The *wrap* is a sentence or statement that ties the copy back into the headline and acts as a conclusion that reinforces the key selling point. For our example, it may read something like this: *We think you'll like doing business with Certified—the interior contractor that's maid to order.*

A small play on words was used to refer back to the headline and leave the reader smiling.

The final part of the body of the ad is the *call to action.* It is a statement, either part of the body or a separate paragraph, that tells the reader what to do. "Call us today," or "For more information contact John Doe," are simple calls to action.

Your advertisement's signature

Make sure that your company name and/or logo, phone number, and web site address are always on your ad and everything else you use for promotion. The name and/or logo will allow readers to make a quick connection if they read only the headline and see the visual. They will at least be able to identify the principal selling point with your company.

The phone number, obviously, gives readers vital information they need in order to contact you. Your web site address, like your phone number, should be on advertisements and every other marketing communications material. The web site will provide them with as much information as a brochure. If the reader visits your site as a result of reading your ad, and actually gets the valuable information you have conveyed about your firm, you will have hit a grand slam.

Designing the ad

There is no room for fudging on any part of an advertisement for which you have enlisted staff members, or hired an outside consultant, or an ad agency at great expense. This is a huge investment in time and money, so don't settle for anything that is lackadaisical or mediocre. If the visual image is important, so are the text, the design, and the overall impression.

The type styles you use for the text and the way in which you lay out the elements of the ad must be contemporary and appealing. If you have the opportunity to study commercial advertising, look for some that were created by one of the best ad agencies in the United States, the one that is owned by David Ogilvy.

David Ogilvy is the dean of contemporary advertising thought. In 1948, he founded Ogilvy & Mather, the renowned firm that has created memorable ads for companies such as American Express, Shell, Sears, Kodak, IBM, Merrill Lynch, and others. Ogilvy now has offices in the United States, Canada, and more than 70 other countries. It was the first agency to be brought to China, Korea, and Vietnam, and is now Asia's largest integrated network. It was also one of the first in Eastern Europe. *Advertising Age* ranked O&M as the #11 agency network worldwide in 2002 with revenue of $589 million. So, any time you get some tips from someone like David Ogilvy, you know they must be good.

Most of the design and writing decisions Ogilvy makes are based on research—what works versus what does not. He says people view ads from the top down. For that reason, he believes the visual should be at the top, with the headline beneath it, and the body copy below. He feels the visual should have a caption because most people will read those. The text should be in a serif type style, flush left and ragged right, because most people are accustomed to reading books and newspapers, which are almost always printed that way. The example in **Figure 9.2** utilizes this format with a slight variation to add interest.

If you simply follow his advice, you won't go wrong. You can make variations to help your ad stand out, but being too offbeat will make it difficult for people to read and understand your ad. And, if you develop a headline and visual combination that work together to convey your key selling point, and write copy so that it succinctly conveys the benefits of your competitive advantages, you will create an advertisement that is much more likely to be effective.

Figure 9.2. People typically look at the photo in an ad, then read the text. Your ads should be laid out to help them.

Radio and television advertising

Writing and designing advertisements for radio and television obviously is different than for print. However, the same steps you take before creating a print ad should be followed before preparing an advertisement for the electronic media.

Television is usually prohibitively expensive because, with the exception of some local cable channels, it reaches such a large audience. For business-to-business advertisers, your money would be wasted advertising on TV because you will reach too many people who would never need your products or services. The audience is too large, it is too diversified, and most are considered consumers of products rather than users of professional services. The only purpose for using radio and television for those in the A/E/C industry would be for name recognition. If you're working with a limited budget, this would not be the best use of your money. However, if your budget is larger, and you want to attract municipalities, counties, or states, this kind of name recognition might be worthwhile. It is for you to decide.

If TV commercials are expensive, radio commercials are relatively inexpensive, but the same scattershot advertising is what you'd get. Most radio stations have tens of thousands of listeners at any given time, many of whom have no need for your services. You must thoughtfully consider the cost for reaching a true prospect before deciding in which media outlet you should advertise. Nevertheless, for name recognition, radio is an excellent medium, and if you can afford it, it might be worth a try.

Effective radio advertising demands good copywriting skills. Because there are no visuals in radio commercials, all of the images must be communicated via the written word and sound effects.

The most important part of a radio ad is the beginning. It must grab the listener's attention. People tend to use radio as background, either while they are driving, cleaning the house, or at work with the volume turned down. Moreover, in the car, people often switch radio stations during commercials.

For that reason, your radio commercial has to have a beginning that makes a listener stop and pay attention. Sometimes it is done with a dramatic statement, and other times it is done with sound effects.

Most radio spots are designed for 60 seconds of airtime. Thirty-second radio commercials are rarely run because most radio stations charge about the same for them as for 60-second spots.

The most effective radio spots are ones that use dialogue between two people. Listeners pay more attention to these. If you use this approach, choose two voices that are sufficiently different from one another.

If you were a local supplier of a nationally distributed product, you might be able to place what is called a *doughnut* commercial. Visualize a doughnut to understand what a doughnut commercial is. It is a studio-produced commercial that has a pre-recorded beginning and end. It may be distributed to local suppliers of the product by the national headquarters of the producer of the product. The middle 10 seconds or so is left blank for you to customize with a localized message. If you listen to the radio, you will hear these often.

Because the greatest benefit of radio is its immediacy—if you want to get a radio commercial on air within an hour, you can usually do it—you may use it to increase last-minute attendance at a special event or lobby for legislation that is about to be voted upon, if that is your particular field. In the A/E/C industry, however, you will need to be creative to determine how radio might work for you. After all, you're not selling carpeting or automobiles, and you're not appealing to Mr. and Mrs. Suburbia.

Radio commercials are often relatively inexpensive to run, so you should thoughtfully consider how they might fit in to your overall marketing communications program. "That efficient highway just completed that takes you from point A to point B was designed and built by XYZ Transportation Construction Company, the company that makes our world better for all of us."

"Take a look at Paradise Mall on Highway 19. Remember when you shop in its elegant and comfortable ambiance that the Goldsmith Venture Group built it."

Television commercials can be the most effective type of advertising because they combine words with visuals. It is for this reason that the Internet attracts so much attention as well.

Although radio taps the particular skills of the copywriter, the visual images usually determine whether a television commercial is successful. Television commercials are similar to print ads to the extent that they rely upon words and images working together to tell a story. The difference is that with television commercials, you tell a story with a *sequence* of visuals and words, whereas with print ads you only have one set of images and words to work with.

Television commercials are created by using *storyboards*. Storyboards are sheets of paper, each with about eight illustrations that look like television screens above boxes for text. Once you have come up with a concept for your commercial, which you do in a similar manner as a print ad, you place a drawing in each TV-screen-like box to depict each scene in your commercial. Under each, you write the text that would accompany the visual. Most storyboards for television commercials have only about a dozen scene changes.

The storyboard is used to present the idea for the commercial. Once the idea is approved, the storyboards are handed over to a producer, who finds the talent for the commercial and hires a director to create the spot.

There are alternatives for companies with smaller budgets. Most television studios let advertisers use their studio to film ads, and some companies use one of their own people as a spokesperson rather than using professional actors. However, be careful with this. We have all seen "homemade" commercials that come off as clumsy and amateurish. A poor commercial can make a company seem ineffectual. Therefore, if you have a small budget and feel that you want to place a television commercial, get the TV station to help you create a tasteful spot that conveys a professional image.

If no one else in your market is using television, you may stand out by trying a commercial on a cable station that may appeal to your target audience. As with radio advertising, it is something for you to consider when planning your marketing communications program. You need an attractive, personable, and professional spokesperson; a clear, straightforward, and professional message; a professional visual, perhaps a photo of a recent project that everyone will recognize. Keep it simple. But remember, a single commercial is a waste of time and money. Repetition is key.

Collateral Material

The term *collateral material* applies to a broad group of marketing communications materials that are used to support the sales process. They are sometimes referred to as sales support material because they are often delivered or sent to a prospect by a sales or business development representative. Primary forms of collateral material are items such as (1) brochures, (2) newsletters, (3) project or product sheets, (4) site signs, and (5) article reprints. Other forms of collateral material may include letters of commendation, video and audiotapes, CD-ROMs or software, or coffee cups, T-shirts, and other giveaways.

The more commonly produced items among the list—brochures, newsletters, and project data sheets—are intended to move the prospect from awareness and interest to desire and action. These items are wasted if they are sent cold to prospects. First, there are far more cost-effective ways to create awareness. Second, most people will not take the time to read a brochure or newsletter if they don't already know something about the company that sent it. The best strategy would be to establish awareness first, through advertising, public relations, or even a letter, before sending a brochure to a prospect.

Following is an explanation of how to best produce these tools. Your own personal taste for design and copywriting style will of course come into play when you create these materials. However, an understanding of the basics of each item's strengths and weaknesses, and some dos and don'ts about how to produce them, will help you create more cost-effective materials that will achieve your intended results.

Brochures

At one point or another, just about every A/E/C contractor finds the need for a corporate brochure. Perhaps you have met someone at a luncheon who expresses interest in your firm's services. You've described some of the projects you have completed and they seem applicable to the prospect's upcoming project. So, the new acquaintance says, "Do you have a brochure?"

Corporate brochures can take many forms. They can be previously printed and ready to take off the shelf, or they can be customized by using a variety of preprinted or computer-generated individual sheets. There are advantages and disadvantages for either method.

Preprinted brochures are easy to use because they are always ready to pull out of a box and send, whereas brochures that need to be assembled require someone's time whenever one is to be sent (see **Figure 9.3**). If you send out more than a couple of brochures a week, customizing brochures can get tedious if you are busy.

Figure 9.3. A preprinted corporate brochure.

Customized brochures offer more flexibility, however. If you prepare a sufficient quantity of different inserts, you will be able to customize your marketing packet to suit the needs of each prospect or proposal. If your basic brochure is standard, the add-ins can be changed as needed, so that your mailer will always be up to date. Continually update the sheets that contain lists of projects completed and names of staff. These need to be current.

However, this flexibility comes at a price. The per-unit cost of individually assembled brochures is much higher than preprinted brochures, which are often purchased in quantities of at least 1,000. Nevertheless, if you have a tight budget, the total cost of producing 50 customized brochures is less than the cost of 1,000 printed brochures. If you don't send out more than ten brochures a month, customizing will probably make more sense for you.

Typically, contractors use a combination of both a preprinted brochure that focuses on selling points that are not likely to change over a few years and individual sheets that profile project types, which gives them the flexibility to update information as their situations change.

Preprinted brochures have a cover that typically includes the company's name and an eye-catching graphic element like a photo of a notable project or an artistic image of a construction site at sunset (see **Figure 9.4**). Whatever is chosen for the cover, it must attract attention and express the selling points you want to convey.

Most brochures are organized using an outline that includes an introduction, the body—usually a presentation of your competitive advantages, which you identified when you prepared your creative platform—and a conclusion. The length of the brochure depends on how much space you need to present the essential items in your outline.

*Figure 9.4. Preprinted brochures typically include the company's **name** and an eye-catching graphic.*

"We have worked with Hensel Phelps on 22 projects valued at more than $550 million. The thing that has impressed me the most over this extended association is their uncanny ability to attract, train, and hold what I consider to be some of the most talented people in the construction industry."

*Curt Fentress
Principal
Fentress Bradburn Architects*

12

Figure 9.5. Brochure interiors can vary in format as long as they tell the company's selling points.

Figure 9.5. Brochure interiors can vary in format as long as they tell the company's selling points, (continued).

The brochure developed by the hypothetical interior contractor mentioned earlier might have an outline like this:

1. *Introduction.* An overview describing the company's services and competitive advantages.
2. *Experience.* A description of the benefits of more than 30 years of office renovations.
3. *Project management.* Our flat organization chart, service orientation, and reputation for being nice people to work with saves our clients time and money and minimizes stress.
4. *Quality.* The outstanding projects we build and the numerous awards we have won support our reputation for quality.
5. *Conclusion.* If you need an interior contractor who understands the special requirements of renovation work and want to protect your building investment, we're the right company to do your work.

Developing an outline that conveys your competitive advantages is only one of the many ways to organize a brochure. As an alternative, you may want to organize it by product or project type. For example, a masonry contractor may want to show commercial office buildings, schools, industrial projects, and health care and educational facilities on which it has worked. The text can still focus on selling points. Some brochures focus less on formal organization and story telling and prefer to let the photographs of their products or projects tell the story. They use dramatic photos supported by only a small amount of text (see **Figure 9.5**).

How you decide to organize your brochure is largely subjective. The design decision is based on your personal opinion about how prospects make decisions about selecting a contractor and how you can best portray your competitive advantages. Whatever you decide, there are certain rules you should follow to produce a successful brochure.

1. *Plan.* Once you have developed your marketing communications plan, you will have a good sense of your target audience and competitive advantages. You should know what selling points to communicate and the image you want your company to convey.
2. *Choreograph.* Before you write or design your brochure, you should have a general sense of how you want it to look. Either make an outline or do a thumbnail sketch of which photos will appear on each page and where the text will be placed.
3. *Simplify.* Often, companies want to say everything they can think of about themselves in their brochure. They want to show every variation of project or product they have created. The result is often a cramped, text-heavy brochure that doesn't effectively convey selling points. Instead, simplify. Reduce the number of photos and cut the text. A brochure is intended to make a positive impression, not close a sale. If you get your selling points across,

you will have ample opportunity to meet with a prospect and convince him or her that you are the best choice.

4. *Maximize drama.* People want to be entertained. Your brochure is one of your best opportunities to entertain prospects. Use large, dramatic photographs and short, punchy text.

5. *Minimize input.* Once your company has agreed upon the concept for your brochure in a general sense, minimize the number of people who are to be involved. Everyone has different tastes and opinions, and decisions by committees often produce a hodge-podge of ideas, resulting in a chaotic and muddy end product. What you will end up with will probably be mundane, and a sad waste of money.

6. *Proof it.* You should have several chances to proofread your brochure before it is printed. Make sure you do so very carefully. Small errors are overlooked by even the best proofreaders, so have more than one person go over the copy.   Pay particular attention to people's names, captions, telephone numbers, and fax numbers. You may feel pressured to get the job out quickly, but don't take the risk of letting haste produce waste. Let the brochure sit for a day or two, then have everyone read it again. Once in print, you will be embarrassed if you see an error that could have been avoided.

7. *Manage it.* The last place you want to see mistakes happen are at the printer. Once your brochure is printed, it's too late to correct errors. Invest the time to go to the printer when the brochure is on press and inspect press sheets. Make sure the colors in the photos are exactly the ones you want, and that the quality meets your expectations. Do ask for a blueline. All printers provide them, and it's really your last chance to be certain the piece is exactly what you expected.

If you decide to customize your brochures each time you need to send them out, there are options for producing them. You will probably either print quantities of individual sheets and then, when needed, select the ones that enable you to customize the packet for a particular client; or you will design individual sheets but keep them in your computer for additional customization as needed. When you need to send a brochure, you can then print the sheets you need (see **Figure 9.6** for a sample of such customization).

Figure 9.6. Customized brochures use preprinted individual sheets that can be assembled

Project: Saint Paul
District Heating
System
Our work: Installation,
completed one year
ahead of schedule

Photo by Tim Francisco

*Figure 9.6. Customized brochures use preprinted individual sheets
that can be assembled, (continued).*

O **n Budget, On Time.** ■■ While it's true that we  offer superior materials and workmanship, value-added engineering and an ability to solve problems, these attributes only have meaning if they result in projects that are done on budget and on time. We know that juggling multiple subcontractors and vendors on a project can result in cost overruns and delays. We also know that a one-day or one-week delay can represent a significant cost to you and your clients. ■ A construction site is no place for surprises. That's why everyone at The Egan Companies, from the board room to the back room, is dedicated to delivering consistently accurate project estimates and realistic project phasing. In fact, the majority of our customers say we complete our jobs on schedule and to a higher level of quality when compared to our competitors.* It's not unusual for us to complete jobs weeks, or even months, early and still within budget guidelines.

■ That means whether you're asking for a price on a negotiated contract, or an estimate for a bid-to-spec project, the estimates we present to you have passed the toughest test of all: our stringent standards. That's value we think you'll appreciate.

* Ask an Egan
employee for a
complimentary copy of
The Egan Companies'
Customer Survey.

Figure 9.6. Customized brochures uses preprinted individual sheets that can be assembled when needed, (continued).

LANSDOWNE CONFERENCE CENTER
LANSDOWNE, VIRGINIA

Owner

VMS Lansdowne Development, Inc.
Leesburg, Virginia

Architect

Dewberry & Davis
Fairfax, Virginia

General Contractor

OMNI Construction, Inc.
Bethesda, Maryland

The 10-story Lansdowne Conference Center is a 305-room hotel and resort that includes meeting facilities, two restaurants and a health club. Dynalectric was selected for this high-end project based on its outstanding performance record. The work that was completed by Dynalectric included the installation of two 4,000 amp switchboards, a multiplex addressable voice fire alarm system, and special lighting control and dimming systems. Extensive decorative landscape lighting was installed in large parking areas adjacent to the conference center. This facility is one of the area's most prestigious conference centers.

Figure 9.7. Color-calibrated laser image prints have nearly the quality of printed sheets but can be purchased in small quantities.

In the past, the only way to reproduce good quality photos was to print them on a press. Color printing can be expensive, however, and is not at all cost effective on a unit basis with quantities of less than 500. If you need only 80 individual color sheets at a time, or even 50 to ensure that what you print is never out of date, there are now far more cost-effective alternatives than printing on a press.

Calibrated laser image (CLI) prints are color prints produced on a high-quality color laser printer. The quality is nearly as fine as traditional color printing on a press. And yet, the total cost is far less at small quantities.

To produce these CLI prints, you design what is to be printed just as you would design something to be printed on a standard press. Once you design the individual page layouts on the computer using whatever desktop software you like, give it to the firm that creates the CLI prints. The image is transmitted straight from the computer to the laser printer, not printed and then copied on a flatbed copier. The quality is a result of the high-quality computer equipment, high-resolution laser printer, and the ability to calibrate, or control, the colors. (**Figure 9.7** was reproduced from a color copy and although it is shown here in black and white, you can observe that the contrasts are clear and the photograph is sharp.)

CLI prints can be designed and printed in a few days. So, if you have the opportunity to submit a proposal for a stadium, but have no individual sheets that show your stadium experience, you can design and print enough CLI prints to satisfy your needs and do them quickly.

If you keep individual sheets on your computer and print them out when you need them, rather than using preprinted sheets, make sure that the quality of your color printer is sufficient to create the type of quality that befits your company.

Regardless of how you develop your brochure, the rules given above apply. Make sure your brochure clearly communicates your selling points and does so in an attention-getting and memorable fashion.

Newsletters

Newsletters are perhaps the most misunderstood, and yet potentially the most valuable of all collateral material. Unfortunately, when most people think of newsletters they think "junk mail." That is because they are thinking about some of the newsletters they receive, ones that use most of their space boasting about the latest conquests of the firm. Or worse, it devotes space to the outcome of the company's softball team's games, recent weddings, or new births. It's not that these subjects are unimportant. They are important to the employees of the firm but should be reserved only for internal use.

The truth is, most people outside your company don't have the time or interest to read about your successes or personal matters. They do, however, have time to read information that will help them do their jobs better, and that is where good newsletters succeed.

More daunting, however, is receiving a newsletter in the mail that is filled with trivial nonsense, poorly written. Outsiders don't care. You don't endear yourself to them by wasting their time with what they will consider junk! Everyone has too much mail to contend with already and what you will do with a silly newsletter is not make a friend, but an enemy. The last person they will do business with is someone who wastes their time.

Good newsletters make you want to read them. Think of the newsletters you have read. They usually aren't flashy. In fact, slick designs probably make you suspicious about the editorial value.

The newsletters you like will have interesting, substantial, and important content. Perhaps it's financial advice, like that of *The Kiplinger Letter*. Or perhaps it's a collection of thought-provoking vignettes, such as those found in *Bits & Pieces*. They succeed because they don't waste your time telling you about things that aren't of interest to you. They tell you things that help you do your job better or brighten your day. A humorous tidbit or an industry cartoon can do that.

If you send out a company newsletter, it can, and must, do the same thing—offer critical information, educate, enlighten, entertain. If it does, it will be read and saved. And if that happens, it will become a tool that will generate an ongoing source of business because you will have kept your name and information about your competitive advantages visible to your target audience on a regular and ongoing basis.

To create a successful newsletter, you must understand your prospective client's needs. If you took the time to develop a marketing communications plan, you will already know his needs.

Once you understand those needs, you must make every effort to satisfy them. If you are an interior contractor and most of your prospects are end users, give them advice about how to save money by doing their own minor repairs. Or tell them how to figure out how much space they need when they are looking for new office space. Give them a checklist of what they need to do when they move. Give them unit costs for tenant work (see **Figure 9.8**). Giving *free* technical information is always a grabber. The implication is that there is more where that came from, and you are available as a professional information source, for a fee, of course.

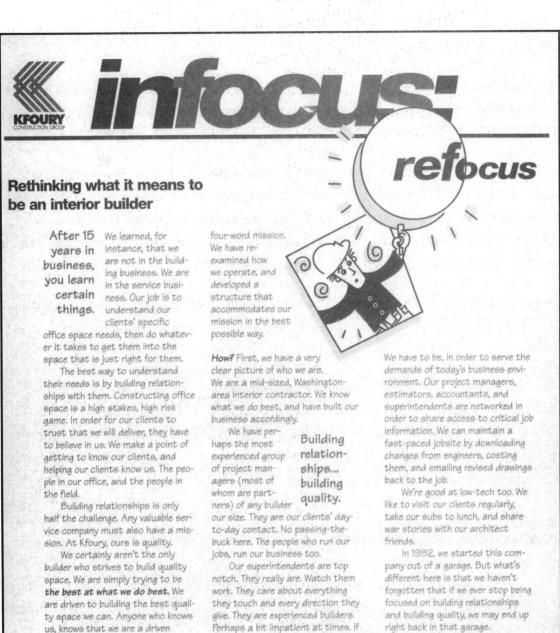

infocus: refocus

Rethinking what it means to be an interior builder

After 15 years in business, you learn certain things. We learned, for instance, that we are not in the building business. We are in the service business. Our job is to understand our clients' specific office space needs, then do whatever it takes to get them into the space that is just right for them.

The best way to understand their needs is by building relationships with them. Constructing office space is a high stakes, high risk game. In order for our clients to trust that we will deliver, they have to believe in us. We make a point of getting to know our clients, and helping our clients know us. The people in our office, and the people in the field.

Building relationships is only half the challenge. Any valuable service company must also have a mission. At Kfoury, ours is quality.

We certainly aren't the only builder who strives to build quality space. We are simply trying to be **the best at what we do best.** We are driven to building the best quality space we can. Anyone who knows us, knows that we are a driven bunch.

"Building relationships...building quality." It sounds simple. It should. We have rededicated ourself to this four-word mission. We have re-examined how we operate, and developed a structure that accommodates our mission in the best possible way.

How? First, we have a very clear picture of who we are. We are a mid-sized, Washington-area interior contractor. We know what we do best, and have built our business accordingly.

We have perhaps the most experienced group of project managers (most of whom are partners) of any builder our size. They are our clients' day-to-day contact. No passing-the-buck here. The people who run our jobs, run our business too.

Our superintendents are top notch. They really are. Watch them work. They care about everything they touch and every direction they give. They are experienced builders. Perhaps a bit impatient at times. If they aren't satisfied with the finish in the board room, they'll strap on a belt and work until it's right.

We're technologically-oriented.

> Building relationships... building quality.

We have to be, in order to serve the demands of today's business environment. Our project managers, estimators, accountants, and superintendents are networked in order to share access to critical job information. We can maintain a fast-paced jobsite by downloading changes from engineers, costing them, and emailing revised drawings back to the job.

We're good at low-tech too. We like to visit our clients regularly, take our subs to lunch, and share war stories with our architect friends.

In 1982, we started this company out of a garage. But what's different here is that we haven't forgotten that if we ever stop being focused on building relationships and building quality, we may end up right back in that garage.

We look forward to continuing to build a mutually satisfying relationship with you in the years ahead. ■

It's easy to contact us...

Call: Tim Reese @ (703) 736-1036   Email: treese@kfoury.com   Fax: (703) 736-0736

Figure 9.8. Newsletters are most effective when they provide information that is of value to the reader.

KFOURY CONSTRUCTION GROUP

Being the best at what we do best

Knowing how not to grow We have built the occasional church or renovated a residence when our personal relationships or client needs dictate. But we are clear in our focus upon being the best at what we do best – building office interiors to the complete satisfaction of our clients.

Rather than dilute our ability by adding peripheral capabilities, we have responded to our clients' evolving needs by establishing separate, independently managed companies.

Jefferson Millwork & Design

The fabrication and installation of millwork is critical to the success of many interior projects. So in 1990, Kfoury Construction Group formed Jefferson Millwork & Design. Jefferson has grown into one of the region's most respected high-end millwork contractors, and its portfolio includes work for some of the area's most notable concerns, like Hogan & Hartson, Merrill Lynch, Sky Tel, Fannie Mae, and the United States Holocaust Memorial Museum, among many others.

ProSum Service Corporation

The vast majority of work tenants need are minor modifications and small repairs – the type of work for which you would not think to turn to a company of Kfoury Construction Group's size.

To meet these everyday needs, Kfoury formed ProSum Service Corporation in 1995. ProSum is staffed to handle small scale office repair and maintenance projects. Fast response and courteous, clean service is their hallmark – the perfect fit for the hectic pace of most businesses today.

By having three separate companies – Kfoury, Jefferson and ProSum – operated and staffed by people with the singular focus of being the best at what they do best, we can give our clients exactly what they need to satisfy their wide ranging construction needs. ■

Jefferson Millwork & Design
44098 Mercure Circle
Suite 115
Sterling, Virginia 20166-2018
Michael Corrigan
General Manager
Mark Howe
Operations Manager
phone (703) 260-3370
fax (703) 260-3371

ProSum Service Corporation
1100 New York Avenue, NW
Washington, DC 20005-3934
Don Manthey
General Manager
phone (202) 408-8800
fax (202) 408-9537

How it all started...

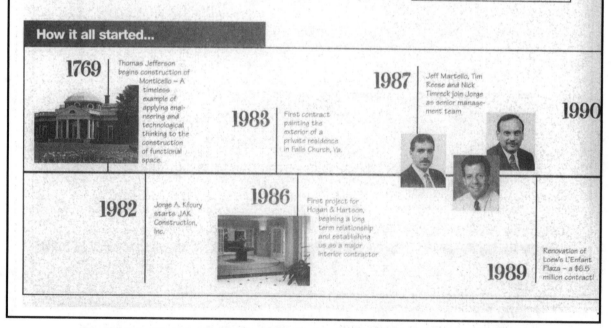

1769 Thomas Jefferson begins construction of Monticello – A timeless example of applying engineering and technological thinking to the construction of functional space.

1982 Jorge A. Kfoury starts JAK Construction, Inc.

1983 First contract painting the exterior of a private residence in Falls Church, Va.

1986 First project for Hogan & Hartson, beginning a long term relationship and establishing us as a major interior contractor

1987 Jeff Martello, Tim Reese and Nick Timreck join Jorge as senior management team

1989 Renovation of Loew's L'Enfant Plaza – a $6.5 million contract!

1990

Figure 9.8. Newsletters are most effective when they provide information that is of value to the reader, (continued).

Kfoury people make the difference

Flat structure keeps the right people accessible

Vertical organizational charts make sense. On paper. People with experience managing others who actually get the work done.

But in a business where the decisions you make this morning have to be put into place this afternoon, you need ready access to decision makers.

Kfoury Construction Group has stripped away layers of management that slow down the flow of communication. Our flat organizational chart provides hands-on access to top managers. Our clients work directly with senior project managers, all of whom have an extraordinary level of experience. And many of whom have ownership in the company.

Name me names

When a project begins, one of six project managers will take responsibility for managing construction, based upon whose particular experience best matches the challenges of the job. Chris Gordon, Mike Hurst, Jeff Martello, Paul Moore, Nick Timreck and Ron Womach — all possess substantial and varied experience.

Chris is a registered architect. Jeff has experience on both sides of the fence — as a developer and a builder. Nick is known as one of the best at preconstruction services in town. Ron, Mike and Paul all have served for years as Kfoury superintendents, estimators and project managers.

We believe you won't find this level of experience and diversity at any other construction firm of our size in the Washington area.

Paul Moore, Chris Gordon and Ron Womach

Our job sites are structured the same way. Clients and subs alike deal directly with one of our superintendents. These are seasoned construction professionals with hands-on responsibility for successfully completing office space.

On the job site

They aren't delegators. They can strap on their belts and work side-by-side with fellow craftsmen to ensure that work is done promptly and efficiently.

Talk to Ken Butts, Ed Comeau, Steve Earley, Paul Fangmeyer, Rick Fortner, Randy Gill, Dan Gonzales, Ralph Hamilton, Glenn McNemar, John Parker, Vern Potter, Dave Stuart or Joel Whipkey. They are passionate about their work. And intent upon keeping our clients happy. ■

Mike Hurst, Jeff Martello and Nick Timreck

1992 — Interior construction begins at Manulife's offices at 1100 New York Avenue

1994 — JAK changes name to Kfoury Construction Group

1995 — After 12 years in Falls Church, Kfoury moves to Reston, Va., into an "owned" building

1996 — ProSum was formed to provide small repair and maintenance for tenants

Kfoury builds 150,000-square-foot headquarters office space for Manor Care

1997 — Ron Womach and Mike Hurst become Partners

2034 — President Clinton (Chelsea, that is), dedicates the Bill Clinton Fast Food Museum, built by Kfoury in one of the last remaining spaces available in the Ronald Reagan Federal Building

Jefferson Millwork & Design established

Figure 9.8. Newsletters are most effective when they provide information that is of value to the reader, (continued).

You should be able to think of many things that will help prospects. Most companies are afraid to do this because they think they are "giving away their work." Perhaps you are, but a small amount of goodwill goes a long way. People will save your helpful newsletters. They will remember your name. And when it comes time to hire a contractor, they will already know your name and some of your competitive advantages. If you feel that by showing them what you do they will be tempted to do it themselves, this is highly unlikely. They probably couldn't do it as well as an expert, and they surely will realize that time is money. You are saving them time, and doing the job expertly as well.

Writing a newsletter is less like writing an advertisement or brochure and more like writing for publicity. Ads and brochures demand brief, concise copywriting and rely more on making impressions than on providing details about your selling points. Publicity writing, like feature articles in newspapers, demands a well-thought-out and complete explanation of your selling points, starting with the most important and ending with the least important.

Headlines are all important for newsletters, just as they are in newspapers. As readers scan the newsletter, it should grab their attention with a headline. Article subheadings and captions are also important because people will usually read them before they read the articles. If you can get your selling points across in your headlines, subheadings, and captions, you will have accomplished a great deal.

Designing a newsletter is more like designing a magazine. The design has to be interesting enough to capture attention but should not detract from the articles. The design needs to help the reader focus on the articles (see **Figure 9.9**).

If the newsletter is mailed folded, a summary of what is inside it should be printed on the outside portion that people see first. That will help them decide to read it if they are scanning their mail and deciding what to keep or toss.

Likewise, if your newsletter is folded into an envelope or mailed in a flat envelope, make certain that the banner, and perhaps a compelling headline, are facing upwards on the flap side, so that this is the first thing the person sees. Stuffing the envelope in the opposite direction can cause the recipient to toss the item into the trash without looking. According to the Direct Marketing Association, the average person takes exactly nine seconds to decide whether to keep or throw away a piece of mail.

Overall, the design elements such as paper, colors, and type styles should be consistent with the design elements used on your other marketing communications materials.

Tysons II, McLean, Virginia

Chapel Valley Landscape Company Receives Two National Environmental Improvement Awards

Chapel Valley Landscape Company was recently awarded two exterior Grand Awards by the Associated Landscape Contractors of America (ALCA) at its 21st Annual Environmental Improvement Awards program in Palm Springs, Ca. This marks the sixth time that Chapel Valley has received a Grand Award from ALCA, the national association's highest honor.

The awards were presented to Landon and Janet Reeve for our firm's landscape contracting work at Tysons II in McLean, Va., and for our landscape design/build services at L'Enfant Plaza in Washington, DC.

Of the 204 projects submitted, only 28 Grand Awards were presented. The association's award's program rewards landscape contracting professionals who execute quality landscaping projects.

Tysons II is a mixed-use development which includes office buildings, parking structures, and the highly acclaimed Galleria at Tysons II retail mall. The project is one of the largest landscape installations completed to date in Northern Virginia, and was coordinated in a tight time frame to accommodate the grand opening of the Galleria. More than 1,000 shade, flowering and evergreen trees, 20,000 lineal feet of irrigation pipe, and in excess of 6,000 cubic yards of soil were installed in six months.

Compounding the tight schedule and large volume of work were the weather conditions faced by our crews. The installation began in 1988 during the most severe summer drought in the Northeast in more than 100 years. Rescheduling to a more optimal planting season was not possible because of the volume of work that needed to be completed before the grand opening of The Galleria in October of that year. Heat emanating from the concrete decks on which the soil was placed was in excess of 130 degrees, and more than 3,000 man-hours, for running three water trucks continuously, seven days a week was needed in order to maintain the life of the plant material.

The sheer size of the project presented the greatest challenges to Chapel Valley crews, according to Tim Nicholson, field coordinator for the Virginia Landscape Branch and the project's foreman at the time. The volume of work necessitated the use of two, and sometimes three, six-person crews working in concert with as many as 25 different construction trades on-

CONTINUED ON PAGE 2

" These awards reflect our clients' commitment to quality."

Chapel Valley Landscape Company

Figure 9.9. The design of a newsletter should grab attention but not take the focus of the reader away from the articles.

LANDSCOPE

L'Enfant Plaza, Washington DC

L'Enfant Plaza, Washington DC

National Awards CONTINUED FROM PAGE 1

site. In addition, because of the weight limitations of working over structure, small one-ton trucks had to be used to move materials instead of the customary cranes.

L'Enfant Plaza presented its own unique challenges. Chapel Valley both designed and installed the landscaping that was a part of the two-year, $35 million renovation of the four-building, 3.2-million-square-foot mixed-use complex in the Federal Triangle area of Washington, D.C. Named after Pierre L'Enfant, the original architect of the city, the project was the largest private development in Washington at the time it was built in the late 1960s.

The focal point of the landscape design was the treatment of the large fountain at the center of the plaza. Measuring 140 feet in diameter, the fountain originally contained water. High maintenance and energy costs prompted the closing of the fountain and the in-filling of landscaping in the 1970s.

A key design objective of the project was to recreate the original intent of the fountain, which was to make an exciting area with bright colors and much movement. We accomplished this through the use of grasses and other perennials, and annuals, as well as ivy hung to resemble the appearance of water flowing over the sides of the fountain. The fountain was not irrigated, however, because the irrigation system installed in the 1970s leaked through the fountain's structure and into a retail shopping mall below grade. Therefore, the system had to be disconnected, and shrubs and perennials that were beautiful but hardy were installed. In addition, more than three hundred 30'-40' trees were removed and replaced with Bradford Pear trees along the Promenade.

According to Chapel Valley Foreman Matt Audia, the biggest challenge his crews faced was keeping his jobsite safe. The high volume of pedestrian traffic using the Promenade, coupled with the need to use heavy equipment like tractors and backhoes, made safety a top concern on the job site.

Since we were incorporated in 1968, Chapel Valley Landscape Company has received more than 100 awards for our landscape contracting or design/build services. "We take great pride in these awards," explained Janet Reeve, vice president of Chapel Valley. "They not only reflect the ability of our craftsmen, but represent our clients' commitment to quality, as well."

Chapel Valley Designs And Installs Garden For Flower And Garden Show

When the Hospital for Sick Children contacted Chapel Valley Landscape Company to design and build an Italian Renaissance-theme garden for the third annual Flower and Garden Show which benefits the hospital, we were delighted to oblige them. The show was held March 15 - 17 at the Georgetown Visitation Preparatory School in Washington, D.C.

The garden was designed by Chapel Valley's Maryland Branch Landscape Architect Eric Rains and Virginia Branch Landscape Architect Craig Klingensmith. They used traditional historical elements, like fountains, stones, urns and evergreens, and integrated them into a courtyard that could be a part of someone's own yard. The urns were filled with flowers arranged by three of Washington's top floral designers.

The garden became an area for people to congregate and use as a reference for their own gardens, and the show was a great success for the hospital.

2.

Figure 9.9. The design of a newsletter should grab attention but not take the focus of the reader away from the articles, (continued).

J. *Landon Reeve IV*

President's Message

It was the Spring of 1977 when Chapel Valley launched its first issue of *Landscope*, a newsletter which was published quarterly for five years, but only sporadically since then. We always received positive feedback about *Landscope*, and felt that we must have been accomplishing our goal of improving the communication between ourselves and the many professionals involved with our industry.

Now, as we have grown and expanded our services, and as our associates and clients have grown busier managing the new challenges of today's marketplace, we feel the need to recommit ourselves to publishing the newsletter on a regular, quarterly basis. This new *Landscope* will provide you with all kinds of information, from stories about our projects and people, to articles about technical advances in our industry and guest columns from industry experts. We hope that *Landscope* will give you insights into our way of doing business, while at the same time provide you with information that will help you do your job better.

I look forward to your comments and input for future articles, and wish you all great success in the coming year.

J. Landon Reeve IV

J. Landon Reeve IV

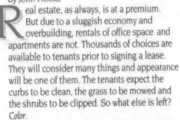

John Hooks

Color Can Make A Difference When Leasing Office Space

By John Hooks

Real estate, as always, is at a premium. But due to a sluggish economy and overbuilding, rentals of office space and apartments are not. Thousands of choices are available to tenants prior to signing a lease. They will consider many things and appearance will be one of them. The tenants expect the curbs to be clean, the grass to be mowed and the shrubs to be clipped. So what else is left? Color.

The addition of seasonal color will command attention to an entry, sign or a particular focal point. Color will greet tenants or guests as they walk from their car to the building. Color will metamorphose a rather common amenity area, such as an outdoor restaurant or jogging trail, into a special one.

Color should be used in impact areas—areas that need the most attention and/or have the most potential number of people viewing it. To be the most effective, color should be used in mass and not as an after thought squeezed in between the turf and the first row of shrubs. Extensive soil preparation must be part of any seasonal color package. Decorative containers planted with seasonal color will soften landscapes and break up large concrete expanses.

A carefully orchestrated and well-maintained seasonal color program can distinguish the ordinary from the extraordinary. Color can and will make the difference.

John Hooks is senior vice president of Post Landscape Atlanta, Post Properties, Inc., which has numerous apartment and commercial properties in Atlanta and one in Fairfax, Va. Chapel Valley, which provides maintenance for the Fairfax property, asked John to write about the value of color. Post Properties is noted for its use of lavish color in landscape with annual flower treatments.

5.

Figure 9.9. The design of a newsletter should grab attention but not take the focus of the reader away from the articles, (continued).

Project or product sheets

For most companies, the primary way to demonstrate their experience is by showing examples of completed projects in a printed format. These are typically produced on 8-1/2 x 11-inch paper and are often called project data sheets, project profiles, or product sheets (see **Figure 9.10**). These are extremely useful sheets. They can be used for magazine or newspaper advertising, in trade publications, framed for your reception area, and utilized in all sorts of ways. Many companies publish four-color volumes of their projects, at very great expense, and send them to prospective clients. You may not want to go that far, but certainly you should be proud of what your company has accomplished, and should make every effort to broadcast your successes far and wide.

What you show depends on what your prospects want to see. If you are a contractor, architect, or engineer and are targeting developers, architects, or general contractors, it is likely that they want to see finished work. Even if you are a specialty subcontractor or a mechanical or electrical engineer, it is often best to show how your work fits into the overall project. You may also want to show a smaller detailed shot of your work product, particularly if it is unique or complex. Largely, however, prospects are interested in seeing if you have relevant experience in projects similar to the one that the company is planning to build. So, showing a completed arena instead of concrete seats will quickly convey your related experience.

The design style of your project sheet can take many forms, depending on the amount of information you prefer to present and the design elements in your other marketing materials. All of your materials should be consistent in style. (If you are mailing out a hodgepodge of materials, all in different styles, do hire a consultant to help you streamline the design of all your offerings so that when others receive them, they will recognize these materials as yours.) Typically, project data sheets include a photo of the completed project plus possibly a detailed photo showing a specialty trade; the name, city, and state of the project; the primary project team members you feel are important to mention; and a description of the project. You may want to include a definition of the project scope, its size, contract value or duration, and a description of how the client benefited by working with your firm.

Your decisions about design and copywriting should be based on the in-house talent available, and the expectations of your prospects. Most consumers of construction materials and services are fairly sophisticated and are accustomed to seeing professional graphic design and well-written text. (Again, if your in-house talent cannot produce top quality materials, do think about hiring a professional graphic designer.)

Lincoln Center

Minneapolis, Minnesota

Construction of this towering 32-story office building with three levels of underground parking was enhanced in several ways by the selection of Ceco as concrete formwork subcontractor. Ceco's use of wide module construction and haunched girders reduced concrete quantities in the floor system and shearwalls of this 820,000-square-foot structure. In addition, larger bays resulted from the long spans of space created by wide modules. All horizontal and vertical formwork was performed by Ceco's able crews who used flying forms to complete a 25,000-square-foot floor plate every six days.

Developer
Lincoln Property Company
Dallas, Texas

Architect
Kohn, Pederson & Fox Associates
New York, New York

Structural Engineer
Brockette, Davis & Drake
    Associates
Dallas, Texas

General Contractor
M.A. Mortensen
Golden Valley, Minnesota

CECO

Figure 9.10. Project data sheets show pictures of projects and provide important information.

In addition to good design and writing, the quality of the photographs you use will have a great impact on the effectiveness of your data sheets. There are many sources of good photos, as you will learn.

How you reproduce your project data sheets depends largely upon the quantity you intend to print. For quantities of 500 or more, traditional press printing is the best option. It will provide the best quality and is competitive on a unit cost basis versus other options. You can, however, produce small quantities by using CLI prints.

Site signs

Site signs could very well be your best form of advertising. They instantly associate you with your work product, are totally credible because you are making no claims about the superiority of your work, as the work is right in front of the viewer. Site signs can be highly visible to a large audience (people walking by, driving by, or passing by in buses), and are essentially free advertising once the sign has been painted and hung. A site sign is something you must do and want to do, in order to identify the building or project.

You should have a printed guide, or *style manual,* that outlines how any size or shape sign you may be able to install on a job site should be reproduced. Every sign should be consistent with every other sign you produce, in size, color, and location on the job site. If all your marketing materials are produced in a particular style, then that style should also be used on your site signs. Consistency is key. This is who you are—by name, logo, type style, color, presentation, layout, etc. Look around you as you drive through your local area, and note the *styles* of gas stations, fast food companies, major chains, the local 7-11, and note how you react to the familiarity of these signs wherever you see them. Have you noticed how instantly recognizable they are, whether they're in your hometown, across the country, or in other countries? That's what you want. Instant recognition. (We are the Quentin Company, that starts with "Q," that rhymes with YOU, and we produce Quality which is what YOU deserve to have!) You needn't be that flippant in your message, but you get the idea. You want people to remember your name!

Any time you are contracted to design or build a project of any kind, you should place the largest sign you can create in as many locations around the job site as possible. Your business is unique in this regard. How many other businesses get the opportunity to advertise their work in progress so blatantly?

Truck and equipment signs are also important because they maintain the same name recognition. You should include dimensions and locations of these signs in your style manual as well. Moreover, make sure your trucks are always well painted and clean. An A/E/C contractor has many more opportunities to attract business as a result of outdoor advertising such as this. You should always take maximum advantage of this kind of name recognition.

As you drive around town, you certainly realize that there is nothing more off-putting than a homemade or poorly produced sign on a dirty truck. Truck advertising counts. Anyone driving by gets a subliminal message that lingers in the brain, more than you could ever imagine. Have your trucks and other vehicles painted by the best advertising and painting contractor you can find. With shabby messengers running around town representing your firm, you can undo a fortune spent in other advertising and never understand why clients might be reluctant to hire your firm. It's that subliminal thing. You can't ignore it.

Article reprints

Having an article printed about you or your company is a tremendous boost to your marketing effort. It has been said that people believe what they read in print ten times more than they believe what you say about yourself in ads or brochures. Therefore, any time you are fortunate enough to have a positive article written about you, or are prominently mentioned in an article, you should get reprints and include them in your marketing packages. Either you, yourself, someone in your communications or marketing department, or a freelance writer can create an appropriate article for you and place it in a publication read by your past or prospective clients.

Some publications will reprint articles for you. They will probably charge a fee. Some will give you permission to copy or reproduce the article. Either way, seize every opportunity to get reprints and use them with your other marketing materials and send them out in all your outgoing mail.

Other forms of collateral materials

Although brochures, newsletters, project or product sheets, site signs, and article reprints are the primary forms of collateral material used by most A/E/C firms, other methods are also used:

- letters of commendation
- video and audio tapes
- CD-ROMs and software
- Coffee cups, T-shirts, and other giveaways that feature your company name

Find a small useful gadget everyone loves, imprint it with your name and logo, and spread it around. Effective items are cables from computer to telephone outlet, miniature calculators, tape measures, scratch pad/ink pen combinations, and staple removers. Think about the items you use every day, and the one you search for in your desk most. All of these can be effective. How you use them depends on their relevance to your type of work and the needs of your target audience.

Testimonials, in the form of letters of commendation, are one of the best ways to promote your services. Readers are more likely to believe what other owners, architects, or contractors say about you. If your clients don't send you letters at the end of a successful project, ask them to write a nice letter. They usually will. These should go in your marketing packages and be used in proposals.

Videotapes may also be useful if the best way to promote your products or services is by showing a project in progress. Still pictures can't capture a special rigging system, for example, but a video may. The only disadvantage of using a video is that most business people don't have video cassette players in their offices, so you will be asking them to take work home, which might be met with some resistance.

As a substitute for video, many firms are producing CD-ROMs. They have sufficient storage capacity to combine large amounts of information, including text, data, graphics, video, and audio. If you are a concrete formwork contractor, for instance, and want to show different forming methods being installed, a CD-ROM is a good option.

You may feel that the best way to illustrate your services, or provide a needed service, is by developing a software program that prospects can load and use on their computers. You may be an interior contractor, for example, and want to produce a software program that allows tenants to plug in square footage and other measurements along with certain materials to develop budgets for construction. Although the information won't be precise enough to develop contracts, it might be another way to portray your expertise and keep your name visible to prospects.

Putting your logo and a tag line on coffee mugs, hats, tee shirts, and other giveaways will also keep your name visible, as long as what you send is useful and attractive enough to keep out of the trash can. If prospects use coffee mugs with your name on them, your name will be on your prospect's desk on a daily basis. Be super smart, and send him a pound of a very special coffee along with the mug. As he drinks his coffee, he may very well be thinking, "Good old Joe. How did he know I like Colombian coffee in the morning?"

Direct Mail

Direct mail promotion is primarily used to encourage the recipient to take action. Although you can send just about anything directly to someone in the mail—like a brochure or other collateral material—traditional direct mail has a specific purpose and a format that is fairly consistent from one piece to the next. A standard direct mail solicitation has four elements:

1. *An attention-getting envelope* that states the key selling point in a compelling way and entices the reader to open it

2. *A personal, subjective letter* written by the head of an organization or someone influential explaining why you will benefit by purchasing the product or contributing to the cause, or whatever the objective is of this letter

3. *An objective, well-written brochure* or pamphlet describing the selling points

4. *A response vehicle,* usually a return card, that allows you to pay for the product or contribute to the cause

Strengths and weaknesses

The strengths and weaknesses of direct mail are quite different from those of advertising. Direct mail is a *narrow-cast* medium. Unlike advertising, which does not give you control of the what people will see your message, with direct mail you can target people who match perfectly with the demographic and psychographic characteristics of your target audience. You can develop a mailing list with the names, titles, addresses, phone numbers, fax, and e-mail addresses of your prospects, either from lists you develop, or lists you have purchased from list brokers.

Therefore, direct mail is best if you have a small, clearly defined target audience, which is typically the case with most A/E/C contractors and subcontractors. Rather than wasting money promoting your products or services to people who have no interest, as may be the case with advertising, direct mail allows you to speak only to people whom you know need what you are selling.

Like advertising, with direct mail you can *control the message.* You write, design, and print it, so you know what it will say. However, also like advertising, direct mail has limited credibility, because people who receive it know that you wrote, designed, and printed it.

Direct mail messages have one advantage, because they have the potential to be *lingering;* in other words, prospects can reread your message as often as they like after receiving your mail. This is why in direct mail you can include more information, which people can use while they work their way through the decision-making process. If they've been offered similar services by others, your mail may be read more than once as they compare the advantages offered to them.

Direct mail has a *high cost per thousand.* It costs more to reach a person via direct mail than by advertising. However, the people who see your direct mail are qualified prospects. With advertising, you are paying to place an ad in a medium that reaches a significant number of people who have no need for your services.

There are two reasons direct mail is so popular in the A/E/C industry. It can be targeted to certain groups, and it can take a prospect through the entire decision-making process, from creating awareness to generating an order.

A good response rate for direct mail is about 1.5 percent, depending on the quality of the message and the complexity of the service being sold.

Creating effective direct mail

Creating effective direct mail requires the same skills as creating effective advertisements and other marketing and promotional materials. You must identify and clearly convey your competitive advantages and be creative enough to design a mailer that has immediate visual appeal.

Writing for direct mail is different from writing for advertising. With direct mail, you typically have more space to explain your benefits. Although the goal of most advertisements is to create awareness and perhaps action, the goal of a direct mailer is to take a prospect from awareness through interest, desire, and action. Therefore, you need to tell a compelling story that will attract attention, explain your selling points, and persuade your prospects to take action.

The typical direct mail piece is mailed in an envelope, but the benefit of direct mail is that you are not constrained by the limitations of page size as you are with advertisements. You can mail anything.

The size or shape of a mailing piece can be creative, as long as it does a good job of leading a prospect through the decision-making process. Boxes and tubes are excellent vehicles for direct mail. You can be assured that they will stand out in a crowded in-box of mail and be opened.

Here's a tip: Unless you're determined to get out a mailer in this coming week, find a box to place near your desk and toss into it every direct mail piece that is sent to you for a month, or six months, if you have the time. When it is time to decide what you want to send, go through them, and see how effective you (and your team) think they are. You may develop some good ideas about what you want to send, or learn what you would never send.

Mailing lists and services

Obviously, one of the keys to creating an effective direct mail program is developing a good mailing list. You can build your own mailing list using personal information manager software such as ACT! or GoldMine, among others. There are many good list managers in the marketplace. This is the most time-consuming way to build a mailing list, but it is also the best way to ensure that the list contains valuable prospects and that the information is accurate. Many firms hire interns to help them build a database. If you do this, check the product periodically to be sure that the information being entered is correct.

There are many resources for gathering names to put on your list. You can sometimes buy lists from trade or professional associations whose members make up your target audience. Many national associations have state or local chapters. See if your area has local offices of associations like American Institute of Architects, American Subcontractors Association, Apartment Owners and Managers Association, Associated Builders & Contractors, Associated General Contractors, Building Owners and Managers Association, Construction Specifications Institute, Design-Build Institute of America, National Association of Home Builders, National Association of Real Estate Investment Trusts, National Multi-Housing Council, or other A/E/C associations. If they do not have local offices, contact the national office to inquire about the availability of lists customized for your area.

Trade and professional associations are exceptional resources for building a database of prospects. There are several directories in your public library that list national and local associations by industry, geographic location, size, and budget. *National Trade and Professional Associations of the United States* and *State and Regional Associations*, both published by Columbia Books, Inc., are excellent resources. Most associations you belong to have member indices you can scour for names to add to your list.

You can also look elsewhere. Most local business publications or business sections of newspapers have periodic lists of companies, like the top 25 property managers or top 100 privately held companies. You can also add to your database information about companies that has been published in these periodicals. Trade magazines have a multitude of ads. Scour these for prospects. The only problem with these is that company names and addresses may be given but names of executives are not. Don't send mail to the XYZ Company without the name of a person. Chances are it will be directed toward the round file.

Most database management software programs give you the option of producing mailing labels. Check the software's user's guide to learn which size and type of label the software can print. If you send labels to a mailing house, they will probably ask for a specific format for their automated labeling machines.

If you don't have the time or resources to develop your own list, there are outstanding resources for purchasing lists. There are dozens of companies called *list brokers* who sell complete mailing lists. They typically have their own databases and have access to other sources, such as subscriber lists for highly targeted magazines and newspapers.

There are many list brokers, such as Dunhill International List Co., Dun & Bradstreet Information Services, and others, which can be found in your Yellow Pages or other directories under "mailing lists." Database management has become so sophisticated that you can select people by almost any demographic or psychographic characteristic, and the list broker can tell you how many people match your criteria in a matter of hours.

Most list brokers sell names for either one-time or unlimited use. It typically costs about twice as much to purchase a list for unlimited use. Most brokers recommend that you buy a new list every year to account for changes in the database. The brokers usually guarantee an accuracy rate of about 95 percent for their lists. Send your mailers first class, so that incorrect addresses will be returned to you. If you find you're getting too many returns, look for another broker.

After you have produced your direct mailer, whether it is printed or assembled in a box, you will send it to a mail shop along with the labels and a check for postage. The mail shop will put the labels on your mailer, sort and bundle them to conform to postal regulations, and deliver them to the post office. These services also can be found in the Yellow Pages under "mailing services."

You should consult with your mail shop before purchasing lists to make sure that the lists are organized and delivered in a format that is most cost effective for them to use without difficulty. Lists can be saved electronically on disks or printed as pressure-sensitive or Cheshire labels.

Publicity

Public relations, or PR, is a broad term that is used to describe the many functions dealing with the public, anything you do or that people in your office do—from the manner in which a receptionist answers the phone to how salespeople are trained to deal with clients or customers, to how job site construction fences are painted. If it is visual or verbal, if it has any contact whatsoever with people outside of your firm, it is *public relations*.

All these elements affect the perception that the public has of your firm, and these elements must be considered part of your overall marketing efforts. For the purpose of this book, however, we will focus on *publicity,* which is how to use the media to communicate information about your company.

To help you compare the value of publicity to that of other forms of marketing communication, such as advertising and direct mail, you must consider its advantages and disadvantages. Like advertising, publicity is seen in a *broadcast* medium. Articles appearing in newspapers or magazines or stories broadcast on radio or television reach a broad audience—all those who read, watch, or listen to the specific medium. Although you cannot specifically control who sees your articles or hears your radio commercials or interviews, you can narrow your efforts by targeting magazines or newspapers that focus on issues of importance to your target audience, such as trade magazines or all-news radio stations.

Publicity's greatest strength is its *credibility*. People typically believe what they read, hear, or see in the media. Unlike advertising or direct mail, most people believe that the information is objective and written by the representatives of the particular medium. This is true even though much of the information about companies in the media is generated by the companies themselves. It has been said that people find articles or news stories in newspapers, magazines, radio or television ten times more credible than advertisements. When you send a letter or brochure, the recipient is well aware that it is subjective. If they see something about you in a news story, the feeling is that an outside person was responsible for that story, and that it is therefore more objective.

The greatest potential disadvantage with publicity is that you *cannot control the message,* as you can in advertising or direct mail. You may send a carefully worded press release to the media and the person who receives it may extract only a small amount of the information. You may provide quotes to a reporter and find them used in a story in a way that does not convey your true intention. The media person can misinterpret what you said, can change it, or slant it, or give it an entirely different spin, and it may appear not just slightly different, but exactly opposite of what you originally said. You have absolutely no control whatsoever over this process, and recanting later will do you little good.

If you are planning to use publicity as part of your marketing mix, you must be prepared for the downside, the risk of misinformation being disseminated, and understand how to deal with it.

Publicity has a very *low cost per thousand* people who are exposed to your message. You have undoubtedly heard publicity referred to as "free advertising." If you can get an article placed in a publication, you pay only whatever it costs you to prepare it, if anything, but not the cost of the space in the publication. The same is true for television or radio. This is an exceptional bargain, if the publicity is positive. Keep in mind, however, that your efforts are never guaranteed. You may write your own releases, or you can pay tens of thousands of dollars to a public relations firm and get *no return on your investment.* There is no guarantee that the magazine, newspaper, radio station, or television station will use your story. However, be aware that there are ways to get your information into the news, or run as a feature, and if you are interested in pursuing this further, make it a point to read *Tell the World! Results-Oriented Public Relations* by Dianne Ludman Frank and Sheryl B. Maibach, published by SMPS. It is an excellent guide on how to go about the process, step by step.

Like advertising, publicity messages are usually fleeting. After they are seen or heard, they are gone. This is particularly true of electronic media such as television or radio. At least with print publicity, the prospect can reread the article. Certain publications, like monthly magazines, have long shelf lives, meaning they are left around the office a long time.

Publicity is excellent for establishing awareness, and sometimes interest, but rarely will it lead to action. That is still best left to other forms of promotion such as direct mail, exhibits at trade shows, telemarketing, the Internet, and directory advertising.

The Internet

More than any other form of marketing communication, the Internet is the broadest of *broadcast* media. Once you post something on the Internet, whether it is an article, a comment on a newsgroup, or a web site, it is available for the entire world to see. Over a billion people now have Internet access, and that number is certain to grow.

There is no way to know or control who will see your web site. It cannot be targeted in the same way as placing an ad in a trade publication. However, unlike the other forms of marketing communications mentioned, the Internet is largely a *self-directed medium*. With the exception of e-mail transmissions, the only way a person can find your information on the Internet is to look for it or stumble across it. You can increase the likelihood that people will see your web site, for example, by placing your web address on all of your other marketing communications materials and registering it with the Internet search engines and directories.

Internet messages are *not necessarily credible.* Like advertising and direct mail, most people view with skepticism claims of superiority that companies make about themselves. Third-party endorsements are always good to add to web sites, brochures, and direct mail. However, also like advertising and direct mail, you can *control the message* you broadcast via the Internet because you write and/or produce it.

Internet marketing has a very *low cost per thousand* people it reaches because the number of potential viewers is in the millions. Unfortunately, few firms who use the Internet for purposes other than commerce, including most firms in the A/E/C industry, know what kind of return on investment they are getting. Only time, experience, and modifications to accommodate user needs will tell whether this is a cost-effective marketing tool.

Another exciting advantage of the Internet is the number of times people can refer to it. If you have an interesting web site that is changed frequently, people will come back to it often. No other marketing communications material can make that claim. Use your imagination and ingenuity and create something so ingenious and useful (like some simple guidelines, tips, suggestions, a chance to acquire information, or offer something free that can be acquired by contacting you) that anyone who sees it once will be curious enough to visit again, and perhaps pick up additional information from it.

For marketers, a great advantage is that you can update a web site whenever anything needs to be changed. You can add and subtract key personnel, change project photos, update descriptions of your products, or modify your client list, all with relative ease.

The Internet is particularly well suited for creating preference and action; however, it is not a very cost-effective way to create awareness because you have no way of controlling who sees it. People who already know about you, either by seeing an ad or hearing a news story, can refer to your web site for more information.

The Internet provides exciting opportunities for you to mix words with still pictures, animation, and audio to present your services in a new and dynamic way.

As in every business in the world, every profession and discipline, there are *tricks of the trade.* There are those who have learned how to navigate the Internet in clever and ingenious ways so as to make the most of the medium. We are not speaking about technical skill, which is something that some of us learn by spending countless hours at a keyboard exploring and experimenting, but what we are talking about is learning to use the Internet as a marketing medium. You may be able to learn some of the tricks of the trade by reading the book *e-Pro Marketing: How A/E/C Professionals Win with the Web,* by Michael T. Kubal, published by SMPS. The book explores how to set up one's web site, what to put on it, what not to put on it, and how to offer free services that will bring people back to the site again and again, and establish your name in their minds as a credible service supplier.

Exhibits

Companies that promote themselves using exhibits do so at either trade shows or consumer shows. The distinction between a trade show and a consumer show is simply that a trade show limits attendance to people who qualify because of their business affiliation, whereas a consumer show is open to the public.

According to industry professional and author Daniel P. Anderson, this difference is important mainly because it means that greater care must be taken at a consumer show to screen out those people who are not good prospects for your services.

Like direct mail, exhibiting at a show theoretically has the ability to move a prospect through the purchase process, from awareness to action. In practice, however, shows are not very good at building awareness on any large scale. Even with a show like *World of Concrete*, which attracts as many as 50,000 people, to create awareness among just 3,000 of these attendees, your exhibit needs to have a measurable effect on one person every 30 seconds. That's a tall order unless you have a very large exhibit.

Although exhibits at shows may have a minor role in creating awareness, properly used they can be highly effective at moving people from the interest stage through desire and action. They also provide an excellent opportunity to screen prospects and build that defined database that is essential if you need to communicate with prospects repeatedly over the long term.

However, without good planning, exhibiting at a show or industry convention can waste money more rapidly than almost any other marketing communications tool. Success with exhibits depends largely on the planning done before the show and the follow-up work done afterward. For instance, if you are offering giveaways with your name, that's good. If you have a large glass bowl with a sign asking for business cards, and have a drawing for a prize, you may get a large stack of cards. If you don't follow those up with a brochure, or a telephone call, you've wasted your time or money. Even though people throw in their cards casually, with perhaps no interest at all, a follow-up call may yield a lead, a new client, or a new friend. Follow up!

Before committing to an exhibit presence at a show or convention, define your objectives precisely and know exactly what target audience you expect to reach at the show. If your objective is to attract clients and you are exhibiting at a *consumer* show, you may end up talking to hundreds of people and giving out hundreds of expensive brochures with absolutely no results. But do you have any solid prospects you can contact after the show? One solution is to hand out only a simple brochure at your booth, but show people a more elaborate piece that you promise to mail them if they give you their address and phone number. Rather than waste your time talking to people who want to discuss your profession but could not possibly be considered prospects, ask a couple of simple questions at the outset to qualify them.

With respect to trade shows, the most effective exhibitors are the ones who recognize that the face-to-face time you get at a show is best used to move people who are already interested in your service because you've contacted them prior to the show. This usually involves using some combination of pre-show advertising, direct mail, and/or telemarketing to generate interest and to get real prospects seeking you out at the show. If you are marketing concrete pavements at an American Association of State Highway and Transportation Officials convention, for example, you know you have succeeded when someone wearing a state department of transportation badge walks up carrying the coupon you have sent out that can be redeemed for a free copy of your pamphlet, "What Every Pavement Engineer Should Know about Designing Permanent Pavements."

If you need to communicate to prospects over the long term, trade show exhibiting provides a good opportunity to add qualified people to your database of prospects and, more importantly, to gather much of the detailed intelligence about each person that you need for effective follow-up. This requires having copies of your data-gathering questionnaires in your booth and creating a situation where people will be comfortable giving you the time and attention required. One device sometimes used for this purpose is a prize drawing where people are required to provide certain information on the entry form.

Amazingly, many exhibitors don't give a thought to post-show follow-up until the show is over. As a result, either no follow-up is attempted or what is done happens long after the momentum created by the show has disappeared. Planning the post-show activity as carefully as the pre-show preparation can prevent this. A friend mentioned a firm that had collected business cards at the show, but in packing up afterward, somehow they disappeared; no one could find them, and no follow-up was ever done. What a waste!

Once you have decided on the show in which to participate, and have developed a strategy for attracting and following up prospects, you must develop an exhibit that will generate traffic. Trade show exhibits are as varied as advertisements, direct mail, and other marketing materials. Your decision must be based on what will most effectively reach your target audience.

With the wide variety of materials at your disposal, your exhibit need not be just a static display of photos and words. Although enlargements of photos and text are inexpensive, they are not very exciting. You can rather easily include a video, PowerPoint, Internet, or interactive CD-ROM presentation that will not only catch people's attention but also give them the kind of information they need to move them through the decision-making process.

Many marketing communications and graphic design firms specialize in trade show marketing, and several of the major exhibit manufacturers offer creative services. You should contact potential vendors well in advance of the show to discuss concepts and costs.

Presentations

A presentation is a form of marketing communications that is delivered in person. This can happen in a group setting, such as a speech at a trade association meeting, or at a one-on-one discussion with a federal procurement official or someone else that you know would be a good candidate for your services.

Either way, giving a presentation can be an intimidating experience for those who aren't accustomed to it. Part of this pressure comes from the expectation that a personal presentation should result in a sale or a commitment of some type. Although the seasoned salesperson doesn't like to admit it, the probability of getting a commitment on a given sales call is usually determined not by the skill of the presenter but by the mindset of the potential client. If the client has been exposed to the right messages and has developed a positive perception of your services prior to your arrival, the rest should be easy. Meeting a potential client at a show after you have been sending him materials, talked to him on the phone, given him samples of information, and pursued him in a friendly manner for months, by the time he stops at your booth, he should be hailed as a valued friend. If you've played your cards right, he will see you in the same light.

All presentations are made easier through careful preparation. If you have been given information about the people to whom you are presenting, you can tailor your presentation to address their needs. In any group presentation, you should make a point of learning who will be in the audience and what level of background they might have regarding your subject.

If you expect to do personal presentations with any frequency, you should become familiar with one of the software packages now available for creating visually exciting presentations. (Microsoft PowerPoint is the best-known software for this purpose.)

Producing Your Marketing Communications Materials

Clearly, there are qualified consultants available who can provide the creative and production services you need to create powerful and effective materials. However, with the basic understanding of marketing communications available to you in this book, you can do much of the work yourself. Either way, by being well prepared, you will save time and money and yield more effective materials because you know your industry, your company, and your competitive advantages better than anyone else.

Following are the services you will need in order to properly execute your marketing communications program. Some of these can easily be done internally, and for some you might be best served getting help from outside consultants.

Research

To quantify the characteristics of your target audience and determine their needs, you will probably need to do some research. There are two kinds of research, *primary* and *secondary*. Primary research is original research that you conduct or hire someone to conduct. It includes tools such as questionnaires, either conducted in person, by mail, or by telephone, or focus groups. Secondary research is gathering data that has already been collected by others, through companies that collect and sell data, statistics, or whatever. Sometimes research can be done by perusing industry journals or magazines.

Developing anything more than very basic questionnaires or focus groups takes professional assistance. Gathering information from these forms of primary research can be expensive, too, so if you want the information you gather to be of value, you need to make sure the research is properly conducted. The questions on questionnaires must be correctly worded so that there is no ambiguity and so that the questions are easy to understand, and the questionnaire must be prepared in such a way as to generate the highest possible response rate. Don't even attempt to put a questionnaire together yourself, unless you've had a good deal of experience doing so. Poorly devised questions will get poor answers and result in faulty data. Mistakes can be made by amateurs, like the time one questionnaire on which a company's staff had worked for weeks went out without a return address!

Focus groups require a trained moderator to ensure that the participants provide as much information as possible. Moreover, it is often better to have someone outside your company moderate so that participants will give more honest answers, knowing that this person is objective.

Primary research is excellent for getting less statistical information, like people's opinions and attitudes. This can prove valuable in helping to determine whether your services will be beneficial to them. Although it is expensive to generate primary research, it is the best alternative for you if the information you need is very specific.

Gathering secondary research is easier to do because it is already available. However, finding the specific information you need is sometimes difficult, in which case you may need outside help. Secondary research usually results in more factual information, like getting names of prospects from existing directories or databases on company size, number of employees, and geographic location, or getting lists from list brokers. Secondary research also can include reading magazine and newspaper articles to learn more about the marketplace, or getting statistical information from the Department of Labor.

Gathering information is essential if you are planning to base your marketing plan and marketing communications materials on facts instead of guesses. Research need not be time consuming or expensive, but it definitely needs to be done.

Planning

Developing a marketing communications plan is something that must be done before you develop advertisements, brochures, direct mail, publicity, or any other promotional effort.

If you need help, consult a firm that calls itself a marketing communications firm, preferably one with experience in your industry. If you cannot find a marketing communications firm, interview advertising agencies, graphic design firms, or public relations firms that have knowledge of your market and ask if they provide communications planning. Either way, make sure the plan clearly identifies your goals and objectives, target audience, and key selling points, and has a strategy that you and your consultant agree will properly achieve your marketing goals.

Strategy

Preparing a creative strategy is perhaps the most challenging part of any marketing communications plan. This is where you decide how you will communicate the benefits of your selling points to the target audience in a way that will achieve your goals and objectives.

Remember that the creative strategy will guide all of your specific tactics, whether they are advertising, a web site, or a publicity campaign. It will be the document that will allow you to assess whether the creative ideas you or your consultants generate are on target. Make sure you put the requisite amount of time into this activity.

Media planning

If you decide to communicate your competitive advantage to prospects through advertising, the first step is determining which medium is best suited to reach your target audience (there may be more than one). Tasks such as selecting the medium (or media, if you decide there should be more than one), developing a schedule of ad insertions, monitoring placements, and managing payments fall under the umbrella term *media planning*.

Effective media planning requires some experience finding the right publications or electronic media, determining which of them delivers the right *reach* and *frequency* to generate results, negotiating rates, and tracking placement. There are plenty of books and resources available to help you learn media planning. However, if you have a large and diversified target audience, you might consider hiring an advertising agency or an independent media buyer to help you.

The advertising agency can help you develop effective advertisements as well as provide the media purchase function, if you need help with both. It will typically charge a creative fee to write and design the ads and then pay the media outlet directly for the cost of placing the ads. In exchange for providing this service, the agency will collect a 15 percent agency commission from the media.

An independent media buyer handles only media planning and will typically negotiate a fee with clients that is less than the 15 percent commission it would get for paying for the placement of ads. This may seem like the best deal, unless the ad agency provides additional services that you need and those services are compensated through the commission. Also, if you need an ad agency to create the ads, it might be easier to deal with just one consultant.

If, however, you determine that you can adequately reach your target audience using one or a few publications, you may want to handle the media planning yourself. Once you have determined the publications and created a schedule, it is not too hard to keep ad placement on track.

First, however, you have to find the right medium or media. Again, if your target audience is either small or well defined, you may already know what publications, radio stations, or television channels reach them. As mentioned before, if you don't know the best ones to use, directories such as *Standard Rate and Data Service* can be found in most libraries; they list and describe each vendor by subject, and provide ad rates and contact information.

You should make a list of several different media outlets that might work for you, then contact them, and meet with an advertising sales representative to learn more about the audience and *demographic profile* (statistical information about their readers, viewers, or listeners) for that medium. Be forewarned that most advertising sales representatives are very good salespeople and can easily persuade you to select their publication, station, or channel. Put together in advance a list of questions you need answered, such as a clear breakdown of paid readers, an editorial calendar that shows what topics are covered, and so on.

Photography

Good-quality photography is essential in selling construction services. A crisp, artistic photograph taken at dusk has far more impact than a washed-out picture shot with a 35mm camera that makes a building look like it is falling in on itself.

If you need photographs for your marketing materials, the first, easiest, and perhaps least painful option is developing a relationship with a professional photographer.

If you want photographs of buildings, *architectural photographers* possess clearly different skills and use different equipment from publicity or product photographers. Their cameras use 4 x 5-inch film, which eliminates vertical distortion, also called "keying," that creates the effect of a building's tilting inward rather than standing straight up. They know how to use natural light, and also know the effects different kinds of interior lights have on film.

If you want shots of people, either on a job site or in an office, you will want to find a photographer who specializes in people. Their skills include capturing people in spontaneous rather than posed settings. In addition, if you need photos for press releases or newsletters, you need a publicity, or "grip and grin" photographer.

Interview photographers before you actually need one. Judge them as you would be judged, by the quality of their finished products. Get references to find out how easy they are to work with. If you like more than one, give each a few assignments and judge the quality and relationship for yourself. They will be representing your firm when they talk to building owners and property managers to gain access to buildings, so you want them to be professional and diplomatic, not temperamental and demanding.

Another option is buying the rights to existing photographs. If you are in a hurry to obtain a photograph, or if you need photographs of projects in different parts of the country and you can't afford to send a photographer to different cities, you may want to see if photos of the projects you want already exist.

The best way to do this is to contact the owner, architect, or general contractor of the project and ask if the project has already been photographed. If it has, you will probably be referred to the photographer. Unless the photographer has given a client unlimited rights to use the photographs, the photographer retains the rights and can sell them to anyone else for a usage fee. Typically, the fee is less than the cost to hire a photographer for original work.

The only problem with this method is that it requires you to make a number of phone calls to track down a photo, and you will not have visual consistency from your various photographs because different cameras, lenses, settings, and film will have been used. You need to weigh your needs and budget in order to judge whether the aesthetic impact of this method will make a difference. It could be that a variety of approaches may actually result in a quite satisfactory effect.

Still another way of obtaining photos is using stock photographs. There are dozens of stock photography houses, many more than mentioned here, such as The Stock Market (www.stockmarketphoto.com), Getty Images (www.gettyimages.com), and Comstock Images (www.comstock.com). They offer printed catalogs you can browse and choose photos from as well as photo collections on CD-ROM, including flat-rate and royalty-free images.

Graphic design and copywriting

Graphic design and copywriting are probably the two most important elements you will need in order to produce effective marketing materials, and the two that you should weigh most carefully in deciding whether to do these tasks with in-house resources or qualified consultants.

We are a visually oriented society. There is no way of getting around this. With the overwhelming assault on our senses from direct mail, advertising, television, e-mail, the Internet, and so on, and the daily distractions in all of our lives, it is increasingly important that the marketing materials you send grab attention and convey your principal selling point quickly. This can best be accomplished through good graphic design and crisp, clear copywriting.

Basically, graphic design works in three stages: concept, design, and layout. The *concept* is the thinking stage. The designer, who thinks visually, works with the copywriter, who thinks verbally, to blend visuals and words together to convey your principal selling point in the most attention-getting manner.

Some concepts are design-driven, whereas others rely more on words. The combination is somewhat subjective and depends on what your creative team thinks will work best. For instance, if your competitive advantage is saving money for your clients, you may develop a direct mailer with the image of George Washington taken from a dollar bill, peeking through a cutout in the envelope with a few powerful words that compel the reader to open the envelope. Upon opening the envelope, the reader finds a crisp dollar bill with text that cleverly tells the prospect how they can get more of these by working with your firm. That is as far as the concept needs to go.

The next stage for the graphic designer is the *design*. Today, design is done on the computer using desktop software. Two commonly used desktop software programs that have all the tools needed to generate the electronic files service bureaus or printers need to create film are QuarkXPress (www.quark.com/products/xpress) and Adobe PageMaker (www.adobe.com). Since new software comes on the market periodically and old software is updated, research on the Internet for what's the latest and best.

Desktop software allows the designer to create page layouts using any dimensions, add text boxes, which are invisible but define spaces for words, and import photographs or other graphic images such as illustrations. The designer will have many typography styles to choose from, most of which can be purchased in packages.

Once you have laid out your text and graphics, the software links them together in a way that allows film to be made properly. It is important to buy desktop software that links images in this way, or else it cannot be used for printing, which renders it essentially useless except for being output on your own laser or ink jet printer.

A graphic designer will design the promotional piece and print it out, usually in full color, to show how the piece will look. If changes are needed, the designer can make them with the software program and then print out a new design.

Once final comments have been made, the designer moves to the *layout* stage. This is where all the remaining pages or pieces of the promotional material are created, based on the approved design. The desktop software then links the pages and images together in the format required by the service bureau or printer.

Concurrently, the copywriter has moved into the second stage as well. After the concept is approved, the text for the piece will be written. The text can be reviewed in manuscript form or be incorporated into the design or layout and reviewed in a more finished fashion.

The availability of desktop software has misled some people into thinking that it gives them design skills. It does not. Desktop software is a tool for the designer, just like T-squares and X-ACTO knives used to be. Because we are a visually oriented society, it is important that the design and writing of your marketing materials be as professional as possible.

You might want to weigh the pros and cons of performing copywriting and design in-house for certain materials, depending on their importance. You may also want to consider having professional designers and writers establish templates for pieces such as newsletters and data sheets, and then have your in-house staff execute layouts.

Whatever you decide, weigh carefully the use of outside experts versus in-house talent to get the right blend of creativity and value in producing your marketing materials.

Web site design and programming

There is a certain amount of computer programming that is required for developing web sites. If you are considering building your own web site, there are many web building packages in the marketplace. Among them are two commonly used off-the-shelf web publishing software packages—Adobe GoLive CS (www.adobe.com) and Microsoft FrontPage (www.microsoft.com). You can place text and visuals on each page and then the software embeds the coding required to make the site work.

Other more sophisticated programs can be used, such as Macromedia Flash (www.macromedia.com/software/flash), The Network Director (www.nrsinc.com/director.php), and Macromedia Authorware (www.macromedia.com/software/authorware), to add more of the "bells and whistles" that many of today's web sites feature. These programs can be used to add higher-end multimedia and interactivity functions to your web site.

HyperText Markup Language (HTML) is the primary code in which web pages are written. Internet browser software, which provides a graphical connection to the Internet, reads the HTML code. Web publishing software will "write" this code for you, through an interface that is similar to desktop publishing software.

Although there are many different types of web browsers available, Netscape Navigator (www.netscape.com) and Microsoft Internet Explorer (www.microsoft.com) are the most commonly used Internet browsers. At a minimum, someone who is developing a web site must have a basic understanding of HTML and how it works. Often, web publishing software will write code that is not interpreted the same by different web browsers, and therefore someone must edit the file at the HTML level (removing or modifying tags, etc.).

Web development firms have the ability to design, develop, and maintain your web site. Simple additions or deletions, however, can be made in-house with just a bit of HTML training and understanding of a web publishing software package. Even a word processor or simple text editor can be used to create or edit your web site. HTML files are, in reality, just text files with an .htm or .html extension.

If you are planning to maintain your web site in-house, you will need to have the ability to transfer your files to and from the server where they are housed. File transfer protocol (FTP) software, such as WS_FTP, must be used to perform this task. In this way, you can simply download the original file (transfer it from the server to your hard drive using the FTP interface), open it in your HTML editing program, make your changes (add a press release, correct a problem with the coding, etc.), and upload it back to the server using FTP.

Service bureaus

Service bureaus are often the first vendors you will use when producing a marketing communications piece. They take electronic files of your marketing piece and convert them to either film or a high-resolution print.

The printer uses the film to create printing plates. High-resolution paper prints are often used for black and white advertisements or copies, or by one-color printers who make plates directly from them. The resolution, measured in dots per inch (dpi), is at least twice as good as most high-quality laser printers. If you do not have photos in your material, the 600-dpi resolution of most laser printers will probably be acceptable.

The qualities to look for in a service bureau are speed and computer skill. Given the deadline orientation of this business, you will usually want your film or print quickly. However, even professional designers sometimes give service bureaus electronic files with missing fonts, bad links, or other technical errors. A good service bureau will call you to let you know what's happening, or if any problems arise, and be able to fix the problems for you.

Printers

There are several different kinds of printers. Each specializes in different types of work, usually in these categories: one- and two-color printers, four-color printers, and web-fed printers. One- and two-color printers should be used for stationery, newsletters, pocket folders, and other materials that are not printed in full color (known as four color). It is usually best to avoid asking a printer who has two-color equipment to print four-color pieces because to do so they have to run a job through a two-color press twice. This is often logistically difficult when trying to align the printing perfectly or to ensure that the job is "in register." For color brochures and direct mailers, it is best to use a printer that has four-color presses. It is called four-color printing because all the color images are created when the paper is run through four rollers on the press, each of which has one of the four primary colors: cyan, magenta, yellow, and black (CMYK). Most four-color printers actually use five- or six-color presses these days. The extra roller is used to put varnish or an additional specified color on the page.

Quality is subjective. On the back of many printers' estimates is a long disclaimer about how they follow printing industry standards. Read it carefully. The agreement is valid even if you haven't read it, just like the small print in an attorney's contract. Know what you're signing up for before you sign. This statement sometimes allows the printer to deliver "pleasing color," which may not really be good enough to "please" you. Understand how your printer defines this and other issues in advance. If you want near-exact matches of your photographs, for instance, you have to make that clear, in writing, right at the beginning of the transaction.

To ensure quality, especially on four-color work, you should ask for a color proof before the entire job is printed. For material printed on press, the proof will be a Chromalin, Iris, or Fuji. These proofs are made from the four pieces of film generated to make printers' plates. The proofs are made using powders instead of ink; therefore the proof is not an exact reproduction of what the printed piece will look like. You can get a good sense of the richness of colors and sharpness of images, but you will not be guaranteed that the final product will look like the proof.

The best way to ensure that the final product meets your expectations is to inspect the job on the press. You will be given a time to go to the printer and will be shown some of the first sheets to come off the press, once the press operator feels that the colors are correct. At that point, you can make adjustments. As long as your recommendations bring the printed piece more carefully in line with the proof or original photos, you won't be charged for these changes. If your recommendations are made to improve or change the original product, you may have to pay for changes. A press check is time well spent, whether your in-house staff is doing it or you are paying a consultant.

Another essential proof is called a blueline, named for the color of the images on the paper. This proof is typically the last proof that you will see before a job goes on press. Although you should have carefully proofed and made any changes to your work before it goes to the printer, the blueline proof gives you one last chance to make any final changes or catch a missed error.

You will find that managing *time* and *cost* are very much like managing the same items for a construction project. You should ask the printer to give you a detailed estimate. It is up to you to evaluate whether it includes all of the elements your project requires. If it does, managing cost is a matter of making sure that there are no unauthorized changes.

In addition, get a written schedule from the printer. Managing a printing schedule is much like managing a construction job site because in either situation unforeseen problems can crop up. Build some flexibility into your schedule to allow for such problems so that you won't be disappointed if your project comes off the press a few days late.

Regardless of whether you work directly with a vendor or subcontract the control function, the key issues are managing quality, time, and cost, any of which can get away from you quickly when you are producing marketing materials.

Vendor management

To ensure that you are satisfied with your marketing communications materials, you should work closely with your vendors to make sure they deliver the quality, price, and schedule that they promised. If an outside graphic design firm or ad agency is creating your material, you will need to decide whether you want to work with vendors or let your consultant do it. Chances are the consultant will have the knowledge and relationships required to ensure success. Your consulting firm will probably charge a production management fee and will mark up the vendor's bill, typically between 20 to 30 percent. It is usually worth the added cost to have an expert handle that aspect of the project to ensure that your entire investment is not lost due to a careless oversight.

However, if you prepare your marketing materials in-house, or if you have someone on your in-house staff with experience in working with vendors, you may decide to work with them directly. You should save money on production management and mark-ups and establish relationships with people whose services you will depend on throughout your career.

For the purpose of this discussion, *vendors* are the people who produce the final product and use equipment rather than the creativity used by designers, writers, photographers, and other creative resources mentioned in this section. Service bureaus and printers are the two types of vendors with whom you will work most often. Other vendors may include color imaging labs, quick print or copy centers, and photograph developers.

Before you begin a relationship with a vendor, you should meet with a sales or customer service representative, review samples of the vendor's work, and contact the references, both those given to you and the companies for whom the samples were done. Ask the vendor's customers questions such as "How do you find the quality of the vendor's work? Does he deliver on time consistently? Does the final bill match the estimate? Does it charge an inordinate amount for customer changes? Is the company easy to work with? Is it flexible? Does it use the latest technology for outputting film, making plates, and proofs?"

Other types of vendors

There are several other types of vendors who supply copies or computer laser prints. Copies might be used for reproducing documents in a proposal, whereas color laser printers would produce CLI prints used for project data sheets and other color output.

A color proof for a CLI print will be the first print itself, so the proof you see should be exactly the same as the finished product. If you are printing a large quantity of CLI prints, it is well worth it to see a proof before printing the entire job.

Seeing a color proof for CLI prints is important because it will vary from the colors on your computer screen. That is because the colors used on computer screens are different from the colors produced from powders, which is how color laser prints are made. By getting a color proof, you can either ensure that you are satisfied or make minor adjustments to the color and brightness of the printed piece.

You will also probably work with photo labs to process your photographs. Here, too, there is a wide range of quality and services. Labs with one-hour processing typically do not produce the kind of quality you will want if you need photo prints to be reproduced in a brochure or newsletter. Such labs use a high-speed machine that does not allow for much color calibration. You should use a custom lab for making prints that will be reproduced in printed material. It will be slower, sometimes taking a full week to develop prints, so allow for the extra time in your production schedule.

Conclusion

Your Role in the Firm and Industry

Whether you are the principal in the firm, the head of the marketing department, or a marketing coordinator, you are a direct link between the client—person or company—that is commissioning someone to create and complete a project and your firm. Your role is critical.

There is no way of minimizing the importance, effect, or value of the industry that creates, supports, and maintains the built environment. Whether it is architecture, engineering, or construction; whether it's landscape design or interior design; whether it's water purification or air purification; whether it's highways, bridges, shopping malls, office buildings, villages, hospitals, schools, vacation site development, or housing complexes; whether it's senior villages, marinas, amusement parks, or stadiums, these jobs are important to the nation. As the world grows smaller, and we enter a new phase of global involvement, we are empowered to help improve countless numbers of areas in foreign countries, bringing water to nations that have none, bringing roads and bridges, building villages, schools and hospitals, in hopes of improving the quality of life for millions.

The structures thus created improve life for everyone, and have a profound effect on the world economy as well. We must never make light of what we do. We create business; we make money. But more important, we are doing work that is beneficial to hundreds of thousands, perhaps millions of people.

You, the marketer, are the link. As you write the proposals, as you design the brochures, as you go to conferences and trade shows and network, as you make phone calls, you are creating the relationships that will allow these marvelous things to happen. If you have confidence in your firm's ability to do a good job, you certainly have the right to say so, and you should.

The authors hope that you have learned a great deal from this book. By all means, as a marketer, you should know what the project manager does. You should know all about the process of putting together a building, or a golf course, or a marina, or a hospital. It will be your job to talk to the project manager of your client's company, and do so intelligently.

Do not think that reading one book will give you all the information you will ever need in order to do your job. Expanding your horizons is important. The authors suggest that you peruse the reading list at the end of this book, and avail yourself of additional information. If you need specialized information about any industry, any discipline, or any technical phase of the engineering or construction process, there are any number of associations dedicated to those disciplines that will be glad to provide the specific information you need. You need to know how to talk the talk. Each industry has its own vocabulary, its own way of expressing ideas. Whatever specific industry or discipline you're in, you must learn the jargon, and what it means.

Above all, as you contemplate the vast and overarching effect of the services your company provides for many people, an effect that multiplies and ripples like a stone thrown into a pond, you should feel pride, pride in your accomplishment.

Every time you bring a new job home, that is an achievement, the beginning of something good. Make sure that the person in charge, whether it's the CEO of the service firm, or the CEO of the client firm, knows that everyone who had anything to do with the project must be thanked. You, as the marketer, can and should have professional photographs taken of the project, not only for future marketing, but also as a tribute to the project and the people who built it. Have the best photograph reproduced on a card, and send it, with written thanks to every person who worked on this project. Send copies to the media. Send copies to everyone you can think of. But do thank the project people, the office people, the designers, the builders, the carpenters, the steelworkers, the painters, the plumbers, the bricklayers, the concrete pourers, the interior designers, the cleaners. Thank them all.

Convey this idea of achievement to your entire team. They have the right to be proud. And so do you. In fact, it's time to celebrate.

References

* *2000 Marketing Salary and Expense Survey.* SMPS, 2000.

* *The 2001–2004 State DOT Market for Design & Construction Firms.* Zweig White, 2001.

* Abramowitz, Ava J. *Architect's Essentials of Contract Negotiation.* John Wiley & Sons, 2002.

* *AEC Web Site Cookbook.* Zweig White, 2003.

* Alexander, David J. *Guide to Winning Federal Government Contracts.* Zweig White, 2002.

AMA. *Marketing Definitions: A Glossary of Marketing Terms.* American Marketing Association, 1960.

Anderson, Daniel P. *How to Promote the World's Greatest Construction Material.* The Aberdeen Group, 1998.

* Anderson, Kristin L. and Carol J. Kerr. *Customer Relationship Management.* McGraw-Hill Trade, 2002.

* Asner, Michael. *Request for Proposal Handbook.* McGraw-Hill Trade, 2000.

Baber, Anne and Lynne Waymon. *Make Your Contacts Count: Networking Know How for Cash, Clients, and Career Success.* AMACOM, 2002.

Bernstein, Nina. "Online, High-Tech Sleuths Find Private Facts." *New York Times,* September 15, 1997, p. A1.

* Bjorseth, Lillian D. *52 Ways to Break the Ice & Target Your Market.* Duoforce Enterprises, Inc., 2002.

* Bjorseth, Lillian D. *Breakthrough Networking: Building Relationships that Last.* Duoforce Enterprises, Inc., 2003.

* Burns, Richard. *The Ultimate A/E/C Marketing Plan: 7 Steps to Your Most Powerful Strategy Ever!* PSMJ, 2001.

References

Butcher, Scott D. "Planning for Marketing: How's Your Map? A Simplified Approach to Developing Winning Marketing Plans." *SMPS Marketer,* October 1997, pp. 4–7.

Campbell, G. Michael. *Bullet Proof Presentations.* Career Press, 2002.

Christensen, Clayton M. "Making Strategy: Learning by Doing." *Harvard Business Review,* November/December 1997, p. 154.

* *Construction Outlook, 2003.* McGraw-Hill, 2003.

Corelli, Christine. *Wake Up and Smell the Competition: They're Closer Than You Think!* Cardinal Publishing, 2000.

* Coxe, Weld. *Marketing Architectural and Engineering Services.* Krieger Publishing Company, 1990.

Crandall, Rick. *Marketing Your Services: For People Who Hate to Sell.* McGraw-Hill Trade, 2003.

D'Amour, Cynthia. *Are You One Relationship Away from Making Big Money?* Jump Start Books, 2003.

* *Networking: The Skill the Schools Forgot to Teach.* Jump Start Books, 1997.

Dawson, Roger. *Secrets of Power Negotiating for Salespeople: Inside Secrets from a Master Negotiator.* Career Press, 2001.

Doherty, Paul. *Cyberplaces: The Internet Guide for Architects, Engineers, & Contractors.* R. S. Means Co., 1997.

Drucker, Peter F. *The Practice of Management.* HarperCollins, 1993 (reissue).

Dutmer, Rick. "Profit Is an Attitude." *FMI Management Letter,* July 1998, pp. 2–3.

* *Fee and Billing Survey of A/E/P & Environmental Consulting Firms.* Zweig White, 2003.

* Frank, Dianne Ludman and Sheryl B. Maibach. *Tell the World! Results-Oriented Public Relations.* SMPS, 2001.

* Friesen, Carl. *The Fame Game: Crafting the "Expert" Article.* SMPS, 2002.

* Gerwick, Ben. *Construction Engineering and Marketing for Major Project Services.* John Wiley & Sons, 1983.

* Harari, Oren Ph.D. *Leapfrogging the Competition: 5 Giant Steps to Becoming a Market Leader.* Prima Lifestyles, 1999.

* Harding, Ford. *Creating Rainmakers: The Manager's Guide to Training Professionals to Attract New Clients.* Adams Media Corporation, 1998.

* *Rain Making: The Professional's Guide to Attracting New Clients.* Adams Media, 1994.

* Henshall, Ruth and Meredith Bena. *Proposals.* SMPS, 1997.

Heselbarth, Rob. "Contractors Must Differentiate to Survive "Century of Consumer.' " *Contractor,* July 1998, p. 3.

Holliday, Micki. *Secrets of Power Presentations: Overcome Your Fear of Public Speaking.* Career Press, 2000.

Holtz, Herman. *The Business Plan Guide for Independent Consultants.* John Wiley & Sons, 1994.

Jones, Gerre. "Defining Marketing." *Professional Marketing Report,* vol. 13, no. 8, May 1989, p. 1.

Kennedy, Michael and Steve Greenberg. *Clientship: Building Client Service Bridges to Profitability.* ACEC, 1998.

* Klein, Christopher. *AEC Press List.* Zweig White, 2002.

* Kliment, Stephen A. *Writing for Design Professionals.* W. W. Norton & Company, 2001.

* Kogan, Raymond, AIA. *Market Research: Intelligence for Your Firm's Future.* SMPS, 1997.

* Kubal, Michael T. *e-Pro Marketing: How A/E/C Professionals Win with the Web.* SMPS, 2001.

References

* Lentz, Kay and Mary E. Rauch, et al. *Winning New Business: A Guide to Making Great Presentations.* SMPS, 2001.

Linn, Charles D. and Clifford A. Pearson. "Lessons from America's Best-Managed Firms." *Architectural Record,* January 1997, pp. 106–117.

Lipe, Jay B. *The Marketing Toolkit for Growing Businesses.* Chammerson Press, 2002.

Lustberg, Arch. *How to Sell Yourself: Winning Techniques for Selling Yourself...Your Ideas...Your Message.* Career Press, 2002.

Luther, William M. *The Marketing Plan: How to Prepare and Implement It.* AMACOM, 2001.

Mathews, Ryan and Watts Wacker. *The Deviant's Advantage: How Fringe Ideas Create Mass Markets.* Crown, 2002.

Maturi, Richard J. "Disney's Legacy Lives." *Industry Week,* July 19, 1993.

McAlister, Hugh. *Speak Easy: Tools for Power Presentations.* Spirit Publishing, 2002.

Miller, Jack. "Develop an Effective Marketing Plan for Your Construction Company." *Concrete Construction,* November 1981, p. 889.

Ogilvy, David. *Ogilvy on Advertising.* Vintage, 1985.

* *Outstanding AEC Marketing Campaigns.* Zweig White, 2001.

* Park, Craig. *Design. Market. Grow!* SMPS, 2002.

Parkinson, Hank. "Consensus: The Key to a Successful Marketing Plan." *Construction Specifier,* vol. 40, January 1987, p. 54.

Phair, M. "Technology and Leadership Mix." *Engineering News-Record,* April 21 1997, p. 19.

* Porter-Roth, Bud. *Proposal Development: How to Respond & Win the Bid.* PSI Research–Oasis Press, 1998.

PSMJ A/E Fees & Pricing Survey. PSMJ/Resources, 2003.

* Quebe, Lisbeth. Plan It: A Down-to-Earth Guide to Market Planning and Budgeting in the Design & Construction Industries. SMPS, 2002.

* *The Marketing Budget.* SMPS, 1991.

Reilly, Tom. *Value-Added Selling: How to Sell More Profitably, Confidently, and Professionally by Competing on Value, Not Price.* McGraw-Hill Trade, 2003.

Renfro, Rebecca M. and Janet Goodman Aubry. *The Marketing Coordinator.* SMPS, 1991.

* Rosen, Emanuel. *The Anatomy of Buzz: How to Create Word of Mouth Marketing.* Currency, 2000.

* Rothman, Laura B., et al, ed. *Marketing Survey of A/E/P & Environmental Consulting Firms, 2003.* Zweig White, 2003.

* Safford, Dan. *Proposals: On Target, On Time.* ACEC, 2002.

Sides, Richard. "Marketing with Your Mission Statement." *Construction Marketing Today,* April 1996, p. 14.

Sjodin, Terri L. *New Sales Speak: The 9 Biggest Presentation Mistakes and How to Avoid Them.* John Wiley & Sons, 2001.

* SMPS. *Marketing Handbook for the Design and Construction Professional.* Building News, 2000.

Snyder, David P. *How to Mind-Read Your Customers.* AMACOM, 2001.

Stasiowiski, Frank. *Chesapeake Marketer,* Society of Marketing Professional Services, Fall/Winter 1995.

* *Getting Paid What You're Worth: How to Effectively Price Your AEC Services.* PSMJ, 2001.

* Steinberg, Marcy. *Inside Scoop: Proposals & Interviews from the Client's Perspective.* SMPS, 2003.

Stone, David A. *Art & Science of Pricing.* FMI, 2002.

Negotiation Waltz. FMI, 2002.

* *Marketing in the 21st Century for Design Professionals.* ACEC, 2002.

* *Wired! How to Crawl Inside Your Client's Mind for Success in Business Development.* ACEC, 2000.

Trout, Jack. *Differentiate or Die: Survival in our Era of Killer Competition.* John Wiley & Sons, 2000.

* Tuminello, Randy. *What You Need to Know About Doughnuts.* SMPS, 2003.

* Valence, Jean R. *Architect's Essentials of Professional Development.* John Wiley & Sons, 2003.

Volkema, Roger J. *The Negotiation Toolkit: How to Get Exactly What You Want in Any Business or Personal Situation.* AMACOM, 1999.

* *Winning Proposals: How to Build Proposals for Extreme Impact.* PSMJ, 2001.

Yeh, Judy and Allison Tilly Carswell, ed. *The Little Black Book: A/E/C Marketer's Desk Reference.* PSMJ, 2001.

Ziglar, Zig. *Reaching the Top.* Budget Book Service, 1997.

* *Indicates publications available through SMPS.*

Index